Gardens by the Sea

GARDENS BY THE SEA

Alexandra d'Arnoux, Erica Lennard, and Bruno de Laubadére

Translated by Paul Stuart Rankin

Thames & Hudson

First published in the United Kingdom in 2002 by
Thames & Hudson Ltd, 181A High Holborn, London WC1V 7QX

British Library Cataloguing-in-Publication Data
A catalogue record for this book is available from the British Library

ISBN 0-500-51107-1

Printed and bound in China

All that in this delightful garden grows,

Should happy be, and have immortal bliss.

—EDMUND SPENSER

To the waves of the sea . . .

Acknowledgments

We would like to say how grateful we are to all those who opened their beautiful gardens to us, making it possible for this very special book to come out.

ALEXANDRA D'ARNOUX AND BRUNO DE LAUBADÈRE

To all the people who shared their gardens with us, and more, and to some special friends who helped us along the way: Laurie Frank, Warren and Veronique Bierwirth, Christine Khondjie, Nadia Tazi, and Robert Dash. Special thanks to our agent, Helen Pratt, our editor, Roy Finamore, and our designer, Douglas Riccardi of Memo. And finally, to my husband, Denis Colomb.

ERICA LENNARD

Contents

Introduction   10

CONTEMPORARY GARDENS

A Contemporary Garden in the Mediterranean   16
A Sculptural Landscape   24
A Japanese-Style Garden in Corsica   32
A Garden of Shapes in Sardinia   44
An Andalusian Garden   54
The Garden of the Villa Brazilia   64
A Sculpture Garden Near San Francisco   74

COLLECTORS' GARDENS

Headland Garden   82
Trebah   94
An Exotic Garden   106
Confrontation with Nature   118
A Tropical Garden at the Edge of Etna   132
A Botanical Garden in Portugal   144
Palm Trees in Normandy   156
A Garden of Grasses in Rhode Island   166

PLEASURE GARDENS

A Garden in the Rocks   176
The Charm of Simplicity   186
La Quinta do Muro   196
A Garden of Sand in Tunisia   206
A Virgin Island in Saint-Tropez   216
A Wild Garden in Malibu   224
A Garden Above Big Sur   230

Gardens to Visit   236
Index   237

Introduction

The seaside makes us dream, and the passion for gardens is ever-growing. It was proper, therefore, that sea and garden would one day find themselves side by side. Until recently, seaside gardens were rare. Plants subjected to the heat of the sun, the lashing of winds, and the burning of salt spray most often withered, and the frustrated garden lover usually gave in. Today, heavenly gardens grow with their feet in the water. The marriage of irreconcilables has succeeded well. By what miracle? By the use of a greater array of adaptable species, by a freer employment of

OPPOSITE: *A charming contrast between garden and sea; the boat appears like a mirage.*

enriched soils, by recourse to automatic watering systems, which lessen the bite of the salt, and finally by the perfecting of systems of protection, such as screens of vegetation. In short, where once we found hellish and discouraging effort, now there is pleasure. And what pleasure! For in order to discover these seaside gardens one must travel, as they now flourish everywhere, from the coasts of the Mediterranean to those of the Atlantic and the Pacific. Such ventures also require travel across different cultures, for the spirit of gardens is not the same even on the East and West coasts of the United States. The contemporary sculpture garden near San Francisco is peculiar in form to the culture of that coast. Such a garden would be conceived of differently on the East Coast. And a wild garden in Malibu has nothing in common with a garden of

grasses in Rhode Island—other than proximity to salt water. In England, in Cornwall, as thriving as the tropical garden may be, it has nothing to do with the tropical garden you will find on the island of Ischia in Italy. Or again, in spite of their geographical proximity, the Andalusian garden by the landscape designer Fernando Caruncho is a totally different world—very architectural, self-contained, and Hispano-Moorish in inspiration, imbued with a religious sensuality—than the nearby Quinta Botanica in Portugal, with its extraordinary collection of seaside plants, which has a feel of adventure, the high seas, and the spirit of discovery peculiar to the Portuguese. *When wandering from one garden to another, one passes from one world to another. Going with the flow, one has astonishing encounters: with a vegetable garden in Sardinia located at the heart of a garden shaped into waves by the landscape architect Paolo Perone; with a Japanese-style garden in Corsica by the landscape sculptor Eric Borja, a garden that gives the impression of having been cast off by the ocean like a bottle from the seas to attach itself to this rocky coast of surprising beauty; or with the garden by Oscar Niemeyer in St. Jean-Cap Ferrat on the Cote d'Azur in France. You will meet not only the best landscape designers of our time, at the mercy of the waves, but also the greatest architects for gardens that are inseparable from the houses of which they are the fortunate continuation. *The gardens in these pages are dealt with in *three parts: contemporary gardens, collectors' gardens, and plea-sure gardens. May you have fair winds for the journey, which we hope will be as intoxicating as the sea spray on the American, English, French, Italian, Spanish, Portuguese, and Tunisian coasts. Best regards, as one says lovingly in this so-poetic language that flows like water.*

Contemporary Gardens

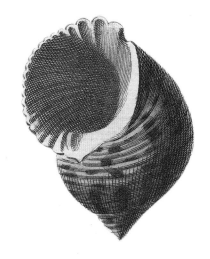

A Contemporary Garden
in the Mediterranean

OPPOSITE: *One glimpses the sea from a terrace paved with pebbles.*

While Paris is still suffering from the chills of March, we embark at Orly for northern Corsica. After only two hours we get off the plane into an atmosphere of springtime, into vegetation completely in flower, with color everywhere and people who exhibit a summerlike relaxation and great kindness. One imagines that crossing the breadth of this mountainous land will be a small expedition. Yet the distance is trivial, and the landscape is captivating. There are slopes everywhere covered with brush and minuscule villages with well-built old stone houses with flat stone roofs, always near a little church and surrounded by palm trees, orange trees, and sometimes vineyards on the hillsides. Through a break between two hills one finally sees the sea. The house and garden we are looking for are superbly situated with a splendid view of the cove and the expanse of smooth blue sea beyond. It is a deep blue on the fringes, from which stands out a chain of mountains crowned by several white clouds. Here one has the impression of arriving at the end of the earth, for everything is wild. The slopes are covered with fragrant underbrush in warm colors, browns moving toward yellow and red. Seduced by this splendid site, still wild at the time, our friends decided to build their house here and surround it with a garden.* "To understand the site, we came and slept on our land! We also spent entire days there, in summer and winter, to*

see where the wind came from and how it turned about. My husband has a true relationship with nature, and before building just anything, this spot became ours physically. Everything is inseparable here, the flora, the fauna, and the people.

"We have succeeded in completely integrating the house with its site. One cannot notice it from any direction, and one has the impression living in it of being inside a landscape. The house is at the same time very architectural and very integrated into the site. It is the same thing with the gardens. They dissolve into the architecture of the house and also, paradoxically, become confused with the surrounding nature." The owner confides in us, "As for the garden, if there is no structure, I have no desire to have plants. It is the architecture of the house that gives the garden its structure. The house extends in very designed levels: terraces, gradations of levels, courts, stairs. Onto them I bring plants and let nature come. Thanks to that, we now have plenty of wild orchids and asphodels—only local plants. I take long walks in the brush and bring back plants that exist nowhere but here.

"It's a complete ecosystem in which one feels like a fish *in* water, totally free. This approach is the opposite of that taken by people who

House and garden are

superbly situated overlooking the gulf.

sweep away nature with a lawn and put in foreign plants. They thus shut themselves off from the outdoors as in a bubble, cutting themselves off from nature and losing its meaning while at the same time claiming a return to basics!

"For me, colors, scents, and tastes are inseparable. Therefore, I made a terraced garden of aromatic plants: thyme, laurel, lavender . . . and of orange and lemon trees. Fruits have something very sexual about them. To pick up an apricot, a peach, or a fig is the height of pleasure. I made an effort so that the garden is as lively in winter as in summer. The rhythms are different and the colors are, too, but it is always in flower."

The first thing to strike one is that the garden seems at the same time both wild and constructed. Having arrived at the side of a hill and opened a creaky old gate, one finds a slope that goes to the edge of the shore. It is punctuated by maritime pines, Aleppo pines, parasol pines, and cypress. Their silhouettes stand out in a lovely manner and define the entire space. Olive trees and masses of oleanders scattered about accentuate this effect of an immense natural garden between the monumental reddish mountain and the almost purple sea. The caretaker's shed is there, hidden behind a vine-covered pergola. We continue along

PRECEDING PAGES: *A partial view of the fruit tree garden going down to the cove.*
ABOVE: *The "wild garden," planted with pines and pink laurels.*
OPPOSITE: *A path, bordered with lavender and myrtle, leads to the sea.*

a low, perfectly straight wall bordered by lavender, which, like a stroke, underlines the blue of the sea with, in the background, the mass of bronze-green mountains, lightly bathed in mist.

One has the impression of being a tightrope walker balancing on a narrow wire between sky and sea, with a light breeze that combines the taste of iodine with the scent of lavender. And like a narrow alley that has the effect of opening to the sky, the road at the end opens suddenly onto the vast landscape.

One then comes across a flight of Italian-style stairs—78 to be exact, says the owner, a believer in *feng shui*—punctuated by pots of red geraniums and cypress and bordered by high walls topped by cascades of oleander. This staircase comes out like a little porch onto an interior courtyard made of little pebbles sunk into cement, giving it the velvety and precious look of shagreen. One used to find these little black pebbles on the beach at Monza. The courtyard retains a certain freshness, and one finds peace here. An amusing detail: One of the side doors in dark wood has the same design as that of an airplane door. Five steps give access to a hanging garden made up of pines and beds. On the right, we find a little room of greenery where several wooden benches have been installed. The spot is protected, isolated, yet at the same time open to the sea.

Along the house one reaches a new terrace. It is marked off by a very low wall that extends as a platform filled with large pebbles, resembling a collection of balls. Numerous orange trees brighten this terrace. The large pebbles capture the strong heat of the afternoon and give it off again in the evening when the temperature drops. Several steps lead by a path to a series of terraces bordered by thyme and lavender and planted alternately with lemon, fig, medlar, and apricot trees. Opposite this slope of cascading terraces that make up this orchard is a wild, virgin mountainside, at the foot of which one discovers a cove of calm water where one comes to bathe in the evening.

On the other side of the house, the salon is extended by a teak deck that gives the feeling of being on the deck of a boat and from which one has a view overlooking the gulf. In the rear, one finds a play of different levels with a gravel floor that opens onto a layer of "shagreen" cement, again punctuated by orange trees in the corners. One is led across these levels to a wild garden made up of pines and oleander that go off into the underbrush, follow the shoreline, and extend out along a path, offering a spectacular walk. One can walk for miles, passing a former Genovese tower and beautiful coves. We are here in the desert of Agriates.

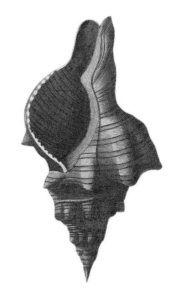

A Sculptural Landscape

We are still in Corsica, the north of the country. In the beginning this garden was nothing but olive trees spreading out along the mountainside that plunges into the sea with a gentle slope. "One day," recounts the owner, "while going by boat to see a painter friend of ours in Corsica, we discovered an immense olive grove between the mountain and the sea. Seduced, we rushed off and had the luck to be able to buy this place. It took us nine months to build the house." The large house is completely integrated into the mountainside by a system of roof terraces transformed into gardens and flanked on the sea side by a pool as blue as the sea, with which it forms a link. In the center of the pool on a kind of island grows a hundred-year-old mastic tree. The garden is extended by a cascade of terraces planted with fruit trees and the olive grove that stretches out to the sea. Under the olive trees grows a lawn with contemporary sculptures placed here and there all over the place. One arrives from the nearest village by a little dirt road all rutted that follows the sea. One happens upon a magnificent allée of hundred-year-old cypress that mounts the mountainside. Several contemporary statues along the roadside seem to await and greet one. Made of raw cement, sometimes pierced by holes, they evoke, in a distant and primitive manner, human silhouettes. Their gray and ocher coloration, like that of the earth, and their surface, like that of tree bark, make them

terrestrial beings, as if they had come from the bowels of the earth, endowed with a soul force. Between the olive trees with their gnarled trunks, which have lived for two centuries and have the spirit of time within them, and the population of cypress, whose silhouettes stand out against the blue sky, one discovers a garden of striking presence and sculptural beauty. In the springtime the lawns form a veritable carpet of green, but as soon as the dry season arrives, the ocher soil reappears and gives it a warm golden tonality.

The house appears at the end of the road. It is the same color as the earth. The porch is marked by the presence of two olive trees, one of which, located in the inner courtyard, has several branches sticking out through an opening. Here, everything is grandiose. The nearby mountain in gray-mauve tones that occasionally has glints approaching pink at dawn is reddish and gold in the evening. The spectacular view of the bay, filled with mists in the morning, is sometimes covered with magnificent cumulus clouds in the afternoon. The vast house is also grandiose, as is this idyllic garden that stretches for acres to the sea, without forgetting the statues of "giants" that participate in the landscape. When the Greeks decided to establish a temple in nature, they chose the most beautiful site, the most beautiful view, because the feeling of fusion with

RIGHT: *The sculptures are like the protective spirits of the garden.*
OPPOSITE: *A spectacular view of the garden planted with olive trees and cypress, looking down toward the Bay of Saint Laurent.*

Here is a garden of striking

presence and sculptural beauty.

nature consecrates the religious link between man and the gods. Here one finds that same dimension. There is something sculptural and mystical in this spot. The garden is as one with the landscape. It is part of our inner life. It is a world in itself, this world to which the Corsicans are attached. The link with this world is almost sacred, vital; it is an amorous link. Here, the earth is not about square feet; it is politics and religion at the same time. "You see," says the owner, "if I prevented my gardener from taking care of the trees and pruning them, from tending the vegetable garden, from going hunting with his dogs, from transplanting trees with me, I would inwardly uproot him. He takes responsibility for the maintenance of these eighteen acres with pride, for it is hard. It takes three days to mow the park in springtime; pruning is done every five days. In the beginning I was afraid, and then I took the bull by the horns. It is on this land that my husband became a sculptor and I am at one with it. To threaten this rapport with the earth of which the gardens are a part by badly conceived tourism would be to put an end to a world, a world linked to this whole Mediterranean culture."

A Japanese-Style
Garden in Corsica

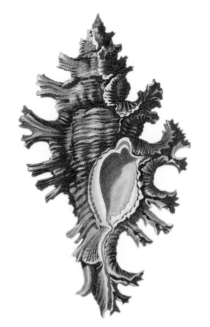

In order to discover the garden created by Erik Borja in the gulf of Porto-Vecchio, we disembark at the airport at Figari in the heat and dust. But the coast we follow soon appears very beautiful, with round rocks and great beaches of fine sand bordered by pines, a nature at the same time gentle and wild. We meet the landscape designer Erik Borja by the pool of a hotel where he has come to wait for us, in order to more easily guide us to the house. He tells us bits and pieces of his life. After the École des Beaux-Arts, he became a sculptor, but following a trip to Japan, he became so fascinated by gardens that he made no other sculpture than that of nature using rocks and the pruning of vegetation. Returning to his property in the Drôme, he began his first Japanese-style garden and finally had the feeling that he had found his true path. Don't the Chinese say, "Life begins the day one begins a garden"? Tall, lean, and gnarled, as if carved in stone, Erik is endowed with a nature both calm and passionate. Today, the invitations to create gardens in France and abroad never end. He is not a designer cast in the mold of a school, but an artist, a true autodidact, original, creative, very gifted at pruning, as well as a fine botanical connoisseur. After his own garden, one of his first commissions was in Corsica. The site was ideal to develop a Japanese-style garden, a garden landscape perfectly integrated with the Mediterranean.*

ABOVE: *The vertical crane island symbolizes the elevation of the soul, while the horizontal tortoise island represents anchoring to the earth.*
OPPOSITE, TOP: *A grass path leads to a juniper pruned to look like a cloud.*
OPPOSITE, BOTTOM: *A dry stone "river."*

"What counts is the site. The landscape here is one of the most beautiful I know. We are at the southern end of the gulf with the Palombago beach and the Benedetto peninsula to the west. Behind is the 'zonza' forest of gigantic and magnificent Corsican pines. Here, therefore, the landscape was the manager of the space. Before creating the garden, a golden rule, I spent more than a year in order to feel how the dominant winds passed in winter, in springtime, and in the summer. To immerse oneself totally in the location is necessary in order to avoid making irreparable mistakes. One needs a certain amount of time to choose exactly what should be saved and to imagine how to treat the vegetation, how it can evolve. I tried to save the beautiful rock formations and to define the spirit of the place relative to these rocks. For here one has the almost perfect prototype with a vertical rock of the crane island, symbol in Japan of the elevation of the soul, and with a nearby horizontal mass, the tortoise island, symbol of our anchoring to the earth. The house had to have a view of these two formations. It also had to rest on an enormous rock facing the entry to the gulf that used to be used as a watch post against Sardinian incursions. It is a guardian rock with a protective influence.

"We wanted a house hidden in the vegetation but with a large opening toward the sea and the best possible highlighting of the existing

34

vegetation. As the land sloped down to the cliff, I first created sloping terraces, a way of capturing the so-precious water. All these improvements took a hundred and thirty truckloads of rocks. The mineral is the bone structure of the site. The second structure is the vegetation. There was an existing vegetation of evergreen oaks, mastic trees, aloes, several junipers, and arbutus, which needed to be remodeled by removal, transplanting, replanting, and pruning. Many species were introduced: palms, olives, and fruit trees. It was also necessary to reshape part of the mass of vegetation by pruning. For that I used three types of pruning: pruning in masses, in flames, and in clouds. There were about fifty evergreen oaks that blocked the view of the sea. It was necessary to lower their profile. I counted on time to affect them. Now this mass that has been regularly pruned gives the impression of never having been taller and of having been shaped by the wind. Its freed branches have a very lovely graphic design and its mass has a very strong presence that falls exactly at eye level, and on the limit it outlines, it has the sea as horizon. This is an example of pruning in mass. I realized in another area pruning in flames, notably with conifers. It is a form of pruning that was held in great esteem in Persian gardens. It is perfectly adapted to conifers like certain yews, which naturally have a plant mass tending toward this

flame form. And finally, pruning in clouds, notably on junipers, arbutus, and olive trees, which separates forms and allows one's sight to pass through the gaps."

Erik Borja has broken all uniformity by cutting three gardens out of the same space, which run one into the next, a bit like in a print with soft focus and successive planes. This depth is one of the great charms of the place. A garden on a single level facing the flat expanse of the sea would be deadly boring. Thus, near the house is a garden with winter fruit trees, with lemons, oranges, figs, a pomegranate tree, and kumquats. There is a secret garden inside a little patio. It is a garden of colors and perfumes, with a tropical note, made up of *Cycas,* ferns, jasmine, and white gardenias. There is also a dry garden located along the wing of the house. One squeezes in among bamboos with fine pointed leaves, following a "water path" made up of little blue pebbles that represent a streaming down from three large stones placed at the base of the trunk of a palm tree.

If the sound of the sea is a constant presence by the bay, in the north, well protected by the walls of the house, it is the sound of a fountain that predominates in the arranged rocks. Children love to play here, inspecting the cracks and having fun with the running water and the

37

PRECEDING PAGES: *From the house, a view toward the west and the Palombaggia coast. At the foot of a protective rock, the plants are all in shades of gray-greens.*
ABOVE: *The house fits perfectly into the landscape.*
OPPOSITE: *A classically pruned tree by the gulf of Palombaggia.*

gravel. Around this fountain daturas and hydrangeas, notably *H. macrophylla* 'Mariesii', proliferate. This grotto is the feminine element of the garden, counterbalanced elsewhere by elements of a phallic nature, like standing rocks, palm trees, and cypress. In spots along the passage aromatic plants proliferate—jasmine, scented geraniums—while another spot in the form of a green clearing, surrounded by pines and scattered with masses of arbutus, plunges down to the sea. Seen from the sea it appears like a wild and natural place, for in Corsica wooded areas punctuated by green fields are common. The lawn yellows in winter, to turn green again in springtime. The wind also regulates this garden. There is an olive tree here, more than a hundred years old, bent over by the east wind. "When there is no wind, we stay in the west. To protect ourselves from the prevailing southwest wind, we stay in a corner where we can dine more agreeably." As for colors, Erik Borja has emphasized gray-greens, blues, and several oranges, with Corsican mimosas, rock roses, and pittosporums. The orientation also regulates the garden: On the seafront are maritime and parasol pines, very hardy junipers, mastic trees, and *Arbutus*. On a lower level one finds creeping Corsican rosemary nicely mixed with *Artemisia* and *Cryptomeria*. Myrtle, rock roses, and lavender are happy here, as are *Acanthus* and *Iris*. Grasses, because of their soft quality, set off the rocks and lend a wild note. To

help the plants withstand the salt spray, a watering system keeps the salt level down.

"My principle has always been to uncover the sea view," continues Erik Borja, "without totally opening it up, for that would be overwhelming. There are openings to the sea everywhere. On the west side one is drawn to the sea by a gentle slope that ends at a balustrade from which one overlooks the gulf. This balustrade is made of copper so that it oxidizes and shows the marks of time. Non-oxidizing materials like aluminum are always very ugly, as they do not evolve." To the east a path opened through the arbutus leads to rocks sunk into the lawn, on which grow mosses or little ferns. One reaches an isolated pergola covered with bignonias, honeysuckle, and passionflowers. Here, away from the house and the sea, and in the shade, one can read or linger in the evening to listen to the charming cheeping of the little toads that live under the rocks.

To find our boat again, we take a little stone staircase that begins at the foot of a two-hundred-year-old juniper, pruned in clouds, that faces the house. The stairs are narrow in ocher-tinted concrete and bordered in whites, bright pink, and purple. The wharf is very wide. In the water the rocks have been cleared to allow the boats to approach. The whole, lit up at night, becomes a swimming pool. Many fish come, attracted by the

What counts is the site.

Above: *A fountain made in the rocks.*

Opposite: *On the headland, the silhouette of a* nigra corsica *pine.*

light. It is a true marriage that Erik Borja has achieved between the earth and the sea. The charm of this house, surrounded by its gardens and planted on magnificent rock formations at the water's surface, as if it were on the back of a whale that emerges from one of the loveliest gulfs of the island, is to offer, after a day out at sea from which one returns intoxicated by the sea spray, another kind of intoxication, that provided by all the sensations peculiar to the earth: the song of the birds in this refuge that is like a nest; the freshness and calm found in the shadows; the colors and scents, rich yet subtle, of the plants. This whole world opposite that of the sea, yet quite complementary, transforms the seaside into a paradise.

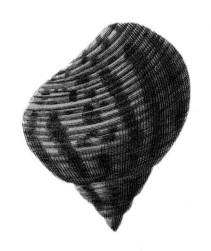

A Garden of Shapes
in Sardinia

We are here near Porto Rotondo, one of the loveliest ports of Sardinia, which was built by a member of our friend's family. She has been coming here for thirty years. Then the land was completely wild, absolutely magnificent, with coasts as far as the eye could see in greens, ocher, and mauve that plunged down into a blue, sometimes violet, sea. This whole place has very fortunately been preserved. But obviously life has greatly changed over the past thirty-five years. The garden is a gently sloping piece of land that ends at the sea, extended by little rocky islands. The wide bay is skirted on both sides in the distance by hills that divide the horizon while overlapping. Our friend, who loves architecture as much as gardens, sought, around twenty years ago, to build a modern house in cement and wood that would be completely integrated with the garden. She discovered a very talented young architect who was the friend of a beginning landscape architect. He is now one of the best there is in Italy: Paolo Perone.* She had the idea of a house with pure lines, just above earth level, with a grassy roof that could serve as a terrace while taking advantage of the rock formations of the land. "I find something of this architecture in Santa Fe, New Mexico, which I am fond of." She also wanted a garden that was not a flower garden, too complicated a thing here given the sometimes scorching sun and the high cost of water. A garden, therefore, that would be composed of*

forms. On the other hand, she absolutely wanted a vegetable garden. "A vegetable garden by the sea is very amusing. To be able to pick tomatoes, green beans, plums, peaches, pears, and apricots is a great pleasure and a delight. What is more refined after a swim in the ocean than to lunch on green beans that have just been picked, and to finish with perfectly ripe fruit?"

There were two months of serious work, with the removal of rocks and the bringing in of earth. "It has only been after fifteen years of waiting that the garden has truly taken over the house. That is because everything is very slow here, with the sun and the wind. The vegetable garden is now part of the life of the house. The children love this garden, as they love the house, because everything is very simple here. The quality of air and the climate are magnificent."

BELOW AND OPPOSITE, TOP: *The vegetable garden repeats the solar shape of the pool. The central basin is covered with water lilies.* OPPOSITE, BOTTOM: *A view of the wild coast.*

The modern house is completely integrated with the garden.

ABOVE: *The house itself seems to be part of the earth, of the garden.*
OPPOSITE, TOP: *The patio, protected from the winds, is planted with* Choisya *and jasmine.*
OPPOSITE, BOTTOM: *A view of the gulf from inside the house.*
OVERLEAF: *The garden spills in waves down to the sea.*

As for the house, large glass bays give the impression that one is in the garden, and at the center of the house a square patio planted with *Choisya* clipped into balls and climbing jasmine, just as fragrant, make the interior-exterior link with the garden. The patio is a delightful place to have breakfast as it is sunny all morning and it is fragrant even before the day becomes warm.

The garden is spread out in front. It is made up of gradual movements of earth, in waves that pour down to the sea, only halted in spots by masses of arbutus, which add a supplementary depth. On the west side, slightly overhanging, by the house, is a swimming pool, spectacular in its simplicity, of a circular, solar form. Three circles, in slight gradations, serve as steps to progressively penetrate the water. They emphasize the design of the pool, giving it the appearance of being a kind of astronomical instrument. On the east side of the garden, the vegetable garden picks up the same circular, solar, astronomical figure. It is made up of a stone wall, eight feet tall, built at a slight angle like a Vauban fortification. The top of the wall is planted with figs and *Arbutus,* which protect the garden from the salt spray. From the center, which is a small pool planted with water lilies, five paths radiate out, each intersected by a median circle that allows one to move about in every direction, and

this division forms "squares" of different plantings: spinach and green beans, tomatoes bordered by roses, aromatic plants, melons, and squash. On the side are several pear and plum trees, but there are also lemon and mandarin orange trees. We are in the vegetable garden of a château, even more attractive because the sea is but yards away! An opening in the wall made by narrow steps, bordered by oleander and *Arbutus* that are like a hedge, leads back to the top of the garden near the house. It is here in the evening, sometimes laden with a basket of still warm fruit, that the owner, delighted at being able to treat several friends, lingers a bit before rejoining everyone.

An Andalusian Garden

Now in Spain, we pass by Seville to find a garden in Sotto Grande, a port situated close to Gibraltar. Leaving Seville, the landscape is rather flat but is soon replaced by lovely little valleys covered with cork oaks where one can often make out horse or bull farms. After one hour on the road, great cumulus clouds on the horizon herald the coast. A road bordered by palms, cypress, and magnificent Ficus *leads to the house we seek. At first glance, its architecture is anonymous. Its lines are rather low and geometric with ocher walls covered with* Bougainvillea. *An ancient and magnificent gate, framed by two large* Phoenix canariensis *palms, marks the entrance. Behind this gate, on either side of a staircase, two great tables of boxwood punctuated at the end by slender cypress are clipped into narrow passages that have the form of Arabic letters. By the justness of the proportions and the sobriety that is exhibited here, the pure lines of great lyric power, one can already guess the style of Fernando Caruncho, one of the finest landscape artists in Spain. It is the peculiar trait of talented artists to immediately know how to mark their style even in a very limited space, as is the case here.* *One enters the garden from a square patio enclosed by walls covered with impeccably clipped ivy, with a soil covered by an arrangement of pink bricks. Long and narrow, they resemble the famous* bejmats *of Morocco, the design of which repeats the latticework on the trunk of a palm*

54

The gardens have a sensory, erotic side.

Above: *Dense boxwoods are punctuated by elegant cypress.*
Opposite: *Carved boxwoods are lyrical, sensual.*

tree. An arched opening cut out of the wall of ivy offers two side passages, each so narrow that it resembles a secret passage or the entrance to a labyrinth. The fleshy ocher color of this opening in the wall of ivy seems like something laid bare. A second opening with black-painted gates gives us a sudden glimpse, like a mirage, of jets of water in a pool bordered by boxwood. This effect of cultivated rigor is suddenly disrupted by the almost erotic unveiling of this garden, which incarnates, in a lyric fashion, beauty and fertility themselves. Thus this opening functions a little like the symbolic passage from the desert to the oasis, from religious asceticism to mystical joy.

The pool is found to be in the shape of a cross, with a square table of boxwood in the center like a little island. These tender green boxwoods, so dense, produce an unreal effect in the blue water. At each corner, a water jet shoots forth and falls into the pool with an excess that is a real celebration. The proportions of the pool are so harmonious that one could imagine them drawn from the golden mean. The masses of boxwood, clipped into diamond points, echo the movement of flight. The water, in its bursting forth and falling back, is a joy; the boxwood, in its sculptural immobility, is calming. The walls here are also covered with ivy and create the effect of the precious upholstery in an antique chest.

ABOVE: *On the perfect lawn, a seventeenth-century statue of a man whose chest calls to mind the shapes of the trimmed box.*
RIGHT: *Lines of box hedges stretch over the grass like motionless waves.*
OPPOSITE: *A pink marble column is a striking exclamation point among the dark green box.*

PRECEDING PAGES: *The abundant foliage of the magnolia contrasts with the gentle lines created by the box.*

ABOVE: *Boxwood "tables" echo the shape of the basin.*

OPPOSITE, LEFT: *Thin sprays of water punctuate the basin.*

OPPOSITE, RIGHT: *Bamboo forms the walls of this garden room paved with pink brick.*

On one side, four olive trees frame a bench placed in the central axis of the pool. A nearby jasmine fills this place of withdrawal with fragrance. In the background, cypress trees emerge from the beds, pointing their heads toward the blue sky. There are no flowers in this garden, but a play of green monochromes: the deep green of the ivy, the dark green of the cypress, the lighter green of the boxwood, the gray-green of the olive trees, the blue-green of the pool.

This sublime enclosed garden opens onto a series of pergolas where there are sofas and armchairs slipcovered in white, which gives the impression of freshness and luxury. When one is seated, one still hears the sound of the jets of water, and against this background noise, the constant muffled plashing of the water in a little pool nearby. In order to stop the frogs from jumping in and croaking all night, the gardener had the idea of pouring in a little copper sulfate, which gives the water a beautiful emerald color and allows those who are not perpetual revelers to get some sleep! Seated, one is at the exact level of the tables of box-wood. One is, at the same time, at the same level as the water of the swimming pool located on one side of the house. Of a pure straight form, the pool marries the geometric lines of the house. It is bordered

by a wall covered with Madagascar jasmine. Two magnificent capitals from columns, white like Carrara marble, lie on the ground. Through the image of bits of ruins they underline the completely designed, laid-out, and clipped character of this place. In April and May it is delicious to bathe here, for leaving the water and stretching out like a lizard in the sun, one smells the sweet fragrance of jasmine. Here, the walls are not flat and abstract. Always colored, they have a sensory dimension.

The house is extended along its length by a covered terrace, punctuated by a play of columns that are hung with white curtains. These curtains sometimes float in the wind and open in a theatrical manner onto a second garden made up of a perfect English-style lawn. It is bordered by boxwood pruned in waves that fan out like breakers dying on the shore. It is at the same time an enclosed garden and a landscape garden because it touches the sea whose movements it takes on while extending the rolling lawns of the nearby golf course. These gardens, with their purity and tremendous power, resemble, in a way, the desert. Yet they have a sensory, erotic side, mixed with the abstraction of geometry. This is the mark of Fernando Caruncho.

The Garden of
the Villa Brazilia

There is no lack of gardens on the Côte d'Azur, but some of them have not aged well. One can count on the fingers of one hand the number of gardens that have remained alive and full of charm, like those of the Waterfelds or the Clos du Perronet, that have improved like a good wine. As for the most recent examples, they are mostly gardens in name only, being limited to lovely lawns planted with cypress, palm trees, and masses of lavender around blue swimming pools. Originality is a rare flower in the gardens of new million-aires (where clichés grow with extreme facility). The garden of the Villa Brazilia is an exception. It is old without being old-fashioned. By some miracle it has remained private and has escaped being turned into a museum. Its owners have highlighted its still very contemporary allure with exquisite taste, and the villa, having been lived in continuously, cannot be more full of life. It was designed by Oscar Niemeyer, one of the greatest landscape architects of our time, who, in spite of his advanced age, continues to create in Brazil. On the Côte d'Azur, Niemeyer met Ferdinand Bac, one of the best landscape architects of his era who was also a friend of Burle Marx, and Barragan, whom he strongly inspired, and all of whom created a Latin American school. Luckily, when the current owners bought the property, nothing in the gar-den had been seriously disfigured, and they were able to restore the garden. And by choosing the excellent Scottish designer Michael

64

Dynamic curves make

a smile of the garden.

ABOVE: *A Henry Moore bronze soars near a curve of the swimming pool.*
OPPOSITE, LEFT: *Water cascades near the house.*
OPPOSITE, RIGHT: *A potted garden, with plumbago.*
OPPOSITE, BOTTOM: *The many curves are a signature of Oscar Niemeyer.*

Innes, they admirably improved it on a botanical level. They increased the garden by several acres, making it one of the largest on the whole coast, by buying the pine forest that makes up the hill. From the ancient pigeon house, it overlooks the entire sea with an almost 360 degree view. The wild appearance of the pine forest, left as it was, happily balances the Niemeyer garden.

Once past the entrance, facing the delightful Palomba cove, a road leads toward the house, winding through masses of vegetation and palm trees. It is bordered on one side by a bed of blue *Echium,* of *Bacopa* (which are violet flowers with gray-green foliage), of *Gestroemia,* solanums, and *Agapanthus.* Blues are therefore the dominant colors, relieved by several oleanders. On the other side, a magnificent fragrant mimosa appears before several hundred-year-old olive trees mixed with oleanders. Nearby, several palm trees, notably a date palm, have their bases hidden by yuccas and pink hibiscus. Sage, agapanthus and solanums invite one to follow the road to the house.

The house is designed without a frontal façade. Another contemporary characteristic: It is built on the horizontal as if it refused traditional verticality. Open with great bays and all in curves, it blends into the landscape and the vegetation. Eight *Pittosporum,* clipped into balls, nicely mark the entry, framed on one side by a mass of fragrant gardenias and

ABOVE: *A small Impressionist lavender garden facing the sea.*
RIGHT: *The lines of the pool, of the shore, of the horizon combine to create an abstract composition.*

on the other side by a jasmine. Near a *Magnolia grandiflora,* which gives off a sweet fragrance when it is in bloom, is a bed of cestrum, which is very fragrant at night.

A paved path goes around the house, the walls of which are covered by jasmine and bordered by masses of hydrangea. It leads to a graveled courtyard, alongside a wall completely covered by a totally magnificent carmine red bougainvillea, which seems to burn in the evening's golden light. Scattered at its feet are *Erigeron,* a kind of minuscule pink-and-white daisy, very delicate looking but extremely hardy. At the angle of the opposite wall in front of a climbing jasmine, a camphor tree stretches out its pale green foliage. Opposite, a service annex, also all in curves, cleverly hides a vegetable and fruit garden on its roof terrace. Also nearby are fruit trees: figs and other treats. Two frangipanis with a

BELOW: *Trees frame the back of the house.*
OPPOSITE: *The pool house, with its ceramic walls.*

marvelous perfume are also planted there. One is surprised and amused to find Christmas ornaments perched atop tall stalks, placed by the owner's wife (who is originally from Austria), to recall happy memories and because they are the very symbol of abundance.

A path that winds under the shadows of large pines lets one see the blue of the sea in the background. One first comes upon a pine forest carpeted by a lawn striped with shadows that slowly descends to the shore; on the left, one sees a pavilion with walls of white faience speckled with blue, all in length and in curves, around a swimming pool. The ground slopes down in gentle waves. Even the waters of the swimming pool, by a play of light and dark blue faience, are separated by a curve that accentuates the desirable confusion between pool and sea. The pool is decorated at the far end by a bronze by Henry Moore, with full round forms.

ABOVE: *A paved path circles the house.*
OPPOSITE: *The beautiful view from the pine forest, looking toward the cove.*

A wide waterway runs from the main house. Having snaked across the garden, it joins the pool. It is adorned with little islands planted with tufts of papyrus and water lilies. Along the path, a delightful wooden pavilion, surrounded by two magnificent *Phoenix canariensis* palms, allows one to rest during this stroll. Along one side of the house beds of grasses, which bend in the wind, are accompanied by diaphanous papyrus and topped by the delicate foliage of a pepper tree, *Schinus molle.* This refined composition is prolonged by a mass of *Grevillea,* whose foliage resembles very fine pine needles scattered with little red flowers. Nothing is more successful than this contrast between the perfect English-style lawn and the wave of grasses and flowers, which have a wild air. This wild side is also found when one takes a little dirt path into the pine forest to reach the pigeon house. Here the master of the house comes to find peace and tranquility. Gradually, as one pushes deeper into the trees, one finds the calm of the forest and scrubland blended together. Here are maritime pines and Aleppo pines, with a more elongated pinecone and grayer bark, several olive trees, myrtle, *Arbutus,* broom, rosemary, and juniper. There are even several heathers, which bloom in the springtime and whose orange flowers are close in color to the ocher soil.

The cove seen through the branches is called the Fossettes. Upon reaching the tower of the pigeon house, fitted out with the greatest sim-

plicity, one feels a happy solitude that ties one to nature, with the blue of the sky, the chirping of the cicadas, the gentleness of the light filtered by the pines. One has the impression of being on an island, for from the tower one sees the sea everywhere. A *Bougainvillea* climbs the walls of the tower. Nothing grows here that has not arrived naturally: lavender, myrtle, rosemary, and *Solanum*. Here, good taste is in naturalness and luxury in simplicity. One goes back down to the house through *Arbutus,* spindle trees, and *Elaeagnus*. Then one again finds the carpet of lawn that stretches in gentle waves toward the sea.

"As soon as I saw it," the mistress of the house tells us, "this garden completely captivated me. Its dynamic and generous curves give me energy. They make a smile of this garden. Everything is imbued with a serenity to which I am very sensitive. Niemeyer operates like an artist. A very strong sense of well-being flows from this garden. I accentuated it by planting fragrant trees and flowers: mimosas, magnolias, jasmines, cestrums, gardenias, and frangipanis. Then, another intoxication: My husband and I love to put contemporary works of art in this garden. They find their place as if they were meant to be here and double our pleasure." On that note, we leave our happy friend attending to one of her favorite occupations: cutting flowers to make bouquets.

A Sculpture Garden
Near San Francisco

We are in a little town by the Pacific, made up of former fishermen's houses transformed into weekend homes by inhabitants of San Francisco who love virgin spaces and the sea. The Brandstens are among these people. Each comes from a wealthy old family in the city and both are known as collectors and generous donors to diverse museums. Occupying one of those rare houses unmarked by any road sign, they have created a garden to display sculpture, Robert Brandsten having a passion for contemporary English sculpture. He chose for this project the architect and landscape architect George Hargreaves, who is head of the department of landscape architecture at Harvard. Hargreaves most recently created the gardens for the Olympic games in Sydney. One arrives at the property by little roads that cross large fields of tall grass, bordering the coast. The grasses are flattened by the wind that also gives a bent-over look to the trees. These, overhanging the cliffs, stand out in silhouette on a blue ground of sea and sky. Getting nearer, one sees at the rear of the house an intriguing white spot in the grass. It is in fact a sculpture arranged, among others, on a well-kept lawn sprinkled with large banks of tall grasses. Very decorative, these banks, with their rounded forms, create the bridge between the sculptures and nature. A metal sculpture, all red, gives the impression of being an airplane on a

74

circular landing pad with its nose pointed toward the sea. The ground, as one advances, is broken into slightly shifting levels that make up vast terraces joined by several steps. These successive levels give structure without breaking with the great fields of wild grasses. Each different sculpture finds its place here without being disturbed by the others. The sculptures are like columns: Their number accentuates their beauty and their presence is that much stronger.

One finds the work of Henry Moore, Barbara Hepworth, Tony Craig, and Richard Long, as well as young artists who were part of the celebrated "Sensation" group. In front of the seaside façade, the crest is made up of underbrush that serves as a windbreak. With the sea, these bushes serve as background for a sculpture made of two curving parts, black on the outside, white on the inside, punctuated by two offset holes. Pure white is the most artificial color in nature and the break caused by this sculpture permits one to better appreciate "natural" nature. Isn't this the highest goal of art? Before this sculpture, one's spirit is guided by the curves of vegetation, then lets itself be transported, to float on the blue waters.

A wooden sculpture rises vertically from a bed in the form of a hedge trimmed into humps. This spot is made up of several of these masses of rounded forms, dotted with little white flowers and pruned in rounds that themselves look like sculptures. A wooden bench integrated into the midst of one of these masses offers a sheltered refuge from the wind where one can sit in the sun and admire the bay that, here, is superb.

OPPOSITE, LEFT: *Peering down over the terraces, one catches sight of the top of the sculptures.*
OPPOSITE, RIGHT: *A neatly pruned flowering bush acts as shelter for this bench.*
OPPOSITE, BOTTOM: *A sculpture rises like a totem from the garden.*
OVERLEAF: *On the terraced garden, an arrangement of contemporary sculptures.*

Collectors' Gardens

Headland Garden

OPPOSITE: *The entrance door opens in a magnificent wall of stones.*

Headland is a little miracle in Cornwall. This unexpected garden was difficult to find. A true garden on the rocks seemed a more suspect mirage to us than an oasis in the middle of the desert. But we set forth on country roads and, after a stop in a pub, board a ferry to cross a little river and arrive on a hill that rises above a little town of white houses and slate roofs where no one knows of a woman with a garden perched on a cliff! Chance guides us to a pretty stone wall embraced by a Hydrangea seemannii *with ravishing little white flowers. Beyond, one can see a flag of the Royal National Lifeboat Institution, which clacks in the wind. An old wooden door is partly open. Before taking the staircase that leads down to the house, one sees a small terraced vegetable garden with a view of the sea. There are fava beans, all kinds of mint, a fig tree, loganberries on the south-facing wall, asparagus, an old pear tree, currant bushes. Everything that has been planted was chosen for pleasure.* A pebbled path leads us to the house. On the ground on a large slate plaque, an arrow indicates North. It is undoubtedly the house of a sailor, who at life's end wished to keep the sea in his sight. At the entrance, logs have been accumulated and carefully stacked. They feed two good fires in the fireplaces inside, which must be delicious on gray seaside days. One senses here the presence of a life oriented toward the sea.*

One senses a life

oriented toward the sea.

ABOVE: *The rocky shore seen from the cliffs.*
OPPOSITE, LEFT: *A sheltered nook overlooking the sound.*
OPPOSITE, RIGHT: *The stair leads to the cove from which one sails off.*
OPPOSITE, BOTTOM: *The steep pathway on the cliff is made up of small gardens.*
OVERLEAF: *The cliff is covered with a profusion of rock plants.*

A large terrace surrounds the house and overlooks the gardens that fall in rather steep cascades, leading to the foot of the cliffs toward a wild cove. The first grassy slope ends with superb Monterey pines, a copper beech prettily linked with a maple, several holly bushes, and a mass of *Elaeagnus* with gray-green foliage. One descends by a little staircase, the banisters of which are covered by honeysuckle and a very prolific *Leucadendron eucalyptifolium*, the flowers not yellow but a lovely bright red. Four landings follow made up of lawns bordered by pines, *Euonymus, Escallonia,* and *Olearia,* which protect them from the north winds. One is separated from the opposite hills by an arm of the sea, which is furrowed by little motor boats returning from the open sea followed by seagulls whose whiteness stands out from the deep blue of the water. On the last landing, several lined-up pines are bordered at their feet by a raised strip where two lightly curving stone benches are surrounded by *Iris japonica* in a dark blue that resembles that of the sea. An area prettily designed in a demilune creates additional depth. The slope ends with raised stones that protect the bench that is backed up against them from the wind; there one can spend hours in the sun. There one can see everything. A large mass of reeds dominates this corner whose solitude, full of charm, it accompanies with the light rustle of its leaves.

ABOVE: *A view out toward
the sound.*
OPPOSITE: *The second door,
leading out to the cliff.*

On the staircase that leads to a lovely door from which one descends
to the cove, large pebbles punctuate each step in an amusing manner.
This door is almost secret, half hidden in the foliage. At the bottom of
the steep staircase that winds around, one discovers a sandy cove in the
midst of beautiful stone foundations. Perched on top of a cliff are the
ruins of an ancient castle covered with ivy. These are the remains of the
castle of Henry VIII and Catherine of Aragon. To the left, the door gives
access to a minuscule landing from which we watch the owners and
their friends embark on a trip in a small boat that they push into the
water.

But the great discovery is a second door, which opens onto a very
steep face of the cliff on the south side. On such a vertical cliff one could
not even imagine the possibility of a garden! But the narrow platforms,
sometimes edged by dry stone walls, follow one after the other, each
offering a spectacular view plunging down to the sea, for here we are
soaring a hundred feet above the water! One could imagine oneself to be
atop a feudal tower on a watch.

Opening the door, one discovers in a very theatrical manner like the
lifting of a curtain, the dizzying void, the sea, and the horizon. At the
foot of the cliff, a little island on which the waves crash forms a rocky
spur from which a chain was stretched to rocks of a neighboring hill to

RIGHT: *The waterway between the port and the sea is lined with fortifications dating from the time of Henry VIII and Catherine of Aragon.* OPPOSITE: *The cliffs seen from the garden.*

prevent the French ships from reaching the port from this arm of the
sea. This chain marked the limits of the port. A cross planted on the little island denotes that in the Middle Ages the port belonged to the abbey
of Tywardreth.

Here, you are seized either by a terrible fear that flattens you against
the rocks and forbids you to move from fear of toppling over, or by an
enthusiasm, unleashed, a lyrical feeling of true love for nature. The first
flower to come into view is the red splash of a poppy that seems so frag-
ile that the first gust of wind would destroy it. On these granite rocks,
colors have a fantastic effect, an astonishing, joyous intensity. Of course,
irises are happy here, as well as lizards. We find a rock covered by thick,
almost woolly moss in a gray-green bleached by the sun. This resistance
and adaptation of vegetation elicits admiration. In the shadow of a wall
of privets, we see a bush of blue *Hebe* 'Thalia', fuchsias, foxgloves that
seem wild, and pretty purple flowers that look like *Convolvulus*.
Geraniums, rock roses, notably the rather rare *Cistus ladanifer* with
crimson-spotted white flowers, do well here, as do *Osteospermum* that
look like white daisies with hearts spotted with blue. Some of them, the
"Sunny Ladies," are mauve. These are very rustic, hardy flowers.

Another little staircase leads to the last and highest "terrace." It is a

Narrow platforms and paths offer spectacular views.

ABOVE: *On the steep slope, an expanse of lawn is planted with palm trees and yuccas.*

OPPOSITE: *A narrow path lined with hedges of thorny shrubs, a perfect barrier against the winds.*

plot of lawn planted with a dozen palms, mostly *Dracaena*. They are accompanied by yuccas and spread about in a very successful effect of perspective. The effect is unreal, strange, dreamlike. One has the impression of a flying carpet, of a little folly transported to the sky. The image of the exotic palm trees and the perfect English lawn, everything is there like a collage with a background of sky and sea together, in a silence punctuated by the cries of seagulls. This sublime tranquility is also felt a little further on, on a stone bench, sunk into the rocks, surrounded by thyme and santolina, before one regretfully leaves this spot, but with joy that one has not missed it.

Trebah

There is nothing more agreeable when traveling from Paris to London than to take the Eurostar. One avoids overcrowded airports, and one disembarks, as from a Rolls Royce, after just having had the time to notice that the skies here are those of the seaside, full of magnificent clouds, with a very changeable and nuanced light, and that the trees in this maritime climate are more magnificent than elsewhere. From London we head south by car toward Cornwall to discover the garden of Trebah, which is typical of this region. A wild air, a spectacular view plunging to the sea, and, due to the presence of the Gulf Stream, a luxurious vegetation with an exotic predominance. On the country roads bordered by wild grasses, one is fascinated by a landscape of hills broken up by hedges arranged like in eighteenth-century paintings. Let us make the introductions, though. Eira and Tony Hibbert became owners of the garden in 1981 and since then have never ceased restoring it with unflagging energy, and a great deal of taste and originality. Without such temperaments, gardens like these that have been forsaken for a long time would end in disorder and disappear forever. The English understood before anyone else that these private initiatives are best for the health of gardens.*

Eira comes from the Bradshaws, an ancient family originally from Northumberland. One of her ancestors was the president of

ABOVE: *In front of the house, a beautiful view looking toward the valley and the sound.*
OPPOSITE: *Perfect specimens from the palm tree collection.*

the court that condemned King Charles and was the first to sign his order of execution! To maintain tradition, each year Eira decapitates the heads of the hydrangeas, which occupy several acres. But you can be sure that this energy in her is mixed with an exquisite sweetness.

The garden was created in 1826 by Charles Fox, member of a famous Quaker family, and held for over a hundred years until 1939 when it then changed hands every six years and suffered terribly, before becoming once again one of the most beautiful gardens in Cornwall.

Leaving the main highway, we take a dirt road bordered by fragrant viburnums, palm trees, and totally astonishing giant *Echium pininana*. They herald the tropical demeanor of the garden. At the last bend of the road we find the house. A large white house with a slate roof and lattice-crossed windows, which, drawn out by a terrace held up by a set of columns, has a rather colonial charm. It dates from the end of the eighteenth century. All around it a sloping lawn ushers in the garden with an abundance of trees and plants that descend to the sea, offering a magnificent view. Eira and Tony greet us with great simplicity and the conversation begins straightaway. In less than two minutes one is convinced that this former soldier with the sly and lively gaze and ready smile, who has told us that here he has found the dreamed-of place that suited him, has in fact found exactly what he sought in order to continue to exercise

One feels totally

immersed in vegetation.

his authoritative sense of organization and to spend the devilish energy absolutely necessary to control this gigantic luxuriant garden.

With the gardens the battle is constant against wind and storms. "The last one eliminated twenty-five percent of the trees. We replaced them with magnolias, oaks, and hollies." There is also the battle against age: the bamboos are one hundred years old, the age at which they begin to flower before dying.

A general look at the garden is enchanting. Palm trees—the oldest in England—emerge from a valley of rhododendrons, a delirium of red, pink, and white flowers. It is bordered by great purple beeches, giant sequoias (Wellingtonia), and umbrella pines whose silhouettes stand out elegantly against the sky. To the left, a mass of *Acacia pravissima* and tree ferns bordered by gigantic gunneras entice one to descend. In the background, Mallard Pond reflects the slopes of blue and white hydrangeas that encircle it. Then the sea appears with, as backdrop, a green hill that rises up and the sky. The view is astonishing. The sea appears as a blue hole, a window at the rear of the luxuriant mass of vegetation, a window through which one sometimes sees passing a white sail, as if in a dream. The view is also astonishing when one is at the bottom and sees on top of the hill the white house standing out against the sky with the colorful mass of thousands of hydrangeas in the foreground surrounded by green foliage as animated as a stratocumulus cloud.

Going deeper into the garden, one feels totally immersed in vegetation. Next we find a grotto, covered in an "ivy" with delicate foliage that is dark green, light green, and golden, from which water streams down into a large oval basin surrounded by tree ferns. Their refined foliage blends wonderfully with that of the blackberry and accentuates the freshness of the atmosphere. Royal carps whirl about in the water. They animate this delicious hidden spot like a silent theater where the gentle rustling of the water breaks a deep silence. In this pleasant shadow, an *Abelia grandiflora*, with pale pink flowers, adds a touch of gaiety.

Following the pathway, we come upon a garden where the sun penetrates strongly with a very Mediterranean tonality. It is a small garden of palm trees, accompanied by yuccas, *Cordyline australis*, and echiums with an underlayer of *Agave, Echeveria glauca*, and *Aloe striatula* with its golden color. In the rocky foundations a myriad of pink and red flowers grow: *Dianthus* 'Laced Monarch', with petals ruffled like a Spanish dress; osteospermums, with gray-green foliage and white and mauve "daisies" marked in their hearts with blue, which make a pretty contrast with several black *Aeonium*. Some would have made such a garden with an effect of "massiculture" in the Napoleon III manner. Here abundance does not kill good taste, and there is always a wild natural air that produces among other things tufts of disheveled grasses.

As one follows the path, which winds as it descends, one almost senses the vegetation growing. One finds oneself at midheight in the midst of *Agapanthus, Iris,* and lilies. The *Iris* are mauve, light-blue, dark-blue, white. There is a completely impressionist atmosphere that would undoubtedly have seduced Monet. A stop lets us make out the sound of a spring that percolates, invisible, at the foot of the plants and which must follow the slope. Turtledoves coo all around, impossible to locate in the foliage. One cannot stop thinking of the painting of Altdorfer that shows a knight drowning in the vegetation of a thick forest.

What is marvelous about this garden is that at each progression one discovers a new and totally different space, while all these spaces blend together. There is diversity and coherence at the same time. Almost every time there is an introductory entrance and an exit; the spaces are admirably structured but in a flowing manner.

OPPOSITE, LEFT: *One spies the house through a break in the trees across the pond.*
OPPOSITE, RIGHT: *Water iris grows in the pond.*
OPPOSITE, BOTTOM: *Eira and Tony Hibbert's eighteenth-century house overlooks the valley and garden.*

ABOVE: *Trebah abounds with extraordinary trees.*
OPPOSITE: *The venerable undergrowth of* Dicksonia squarrosa.

Descending even further, one ends up in undergrowth consisting of tree ferns more than one hundred years old. They are *Dicksonia squarrosa* from New Zealand, brought by the hundreds in 1890 in a sailing ship. "They were then placed in water with a stake," specifies Tony, "and three weeks later they had grown three feet!" A rhododendron has even taken root in the trunk of one of them. This natural grafting makes us think of the story of the stag who during the mating period, having missed his adversary in a ferocious contest, planted his horns in a tree trunk and, being unable to extricate himself, died.

Leaving this very gentle filtered light with moss green and sea green tonalities one discovers the rhododendron valley occupied by a hundred or so different species, some of which reach sixty feet in height. The seeds were gathered during botanical expeditions in the 1890s. It is a magnificent collection and a deluge of flowers. When one reaches the clearing at the heart of the garden, there is a veritable carpet of thirty thousand daffodils, renewed by bluebells later in the spring. Below, one finds a similar expanse of colors, this time thousands of hydrangeas, notably the pink-red 'Parzifal' and 'Ayesha', and the 'Lanarth White'. Of course, Tony developed the collection of bamboo. Numerous varieties are rare, including the Nishida and the nebulosa. But there is also *Himalayacalamus hookerianus* with tiny flowers and *Yushania maling*

from Nepal and *Chusqueaculeou* 'Breviglumis' from Chile. The presentation of this thrilling collection is seductive: The masses form a kind of cabin into which one enters to discover, walking on a very fine carpet of leaves, the different canes. Leaving, one comes face-to-face with a ravishing little pond with water lilies, a couple of mallards, some frogs that jump into the water at our approach, and moorhens that hide themselves.

Beautiful trees are also in abundance. One is in a veritable arboretum. Next to a *Davidia involucrata* is a rather rare pink magnolia. The gardens contain eighteen species of magnolia. One then comes to the *Gunnera* passage. These are giants whose rhubarblike leaves reach from ten to fifteen feet in width! Passing beneath them, one is transformed with the wave of a magic wand into an elf. One enters the world of Gulliver, the land of the fairies of our childhood, fearing immediately coming upon a giant ant or mosquito. The leaves make immense parasols; their phosphorescent green stalks are covered with soft rubbery spines. The urge to touch them is irresistible. Their base consists of a tuft of strangely erotic pink filaments. One is caught in a spider's web that is at once disquieting and amusing. "We feed them well," says Tony, "but if by chance you hear them whistle, move a little faster."

Skirting the pond, edged with water lilies, we near the sea, the sound of the surf already faintly heard. In the pond, the Koi carp grow to nearly

ABOVE: *The flowery path leading from the sea to the house. In the foreground, a Dicksonia.*

RIGHT: *A collection of irises among some echiums and palm trees.*

OPPOSITE: *The Gunnera passage.*

three feet long due to the mild climate. "In order to protect the plants from the salt air, I use a curtain of different varieties of *Senecio: reinholdii, monroi, rotundifolia,*" says Tony. A narrow passage of steps gives access to the beach hemmed in as by two arms by hills with green meadows edged by trees. Several sailboats are anchored. They seem to have always been there and to be part of the landscape, a natural extension of the garden. A swimmer glides silently in the water. On the return, made up of thousands of paths in the undergrowth, of passages and vaults offering ravishing views, one may turn toward the cliff ledge and discover the entire bay. Climbing back toward the house, one hears the feline meowing of several buzzards and one falls dumb with admiration before a group of six *Sequoiadendron giganteum* (Wellingtonia). This extraordinary garden with a junglelike allure is the result of the talent of a botanist and confident taste, with the Quaker strictness of a Fox and the military discipline of Tony, wedded with true tenderness.

Hearing the calls of Eira and Tony inviting us to tea, the celebrated saying of Oscar Wilde comes to mind: "The only way to get rid of temptation is to yield to it." The garden is done with, let's not put off tea!

An Exotic Garden

Tresco is one of the Isles of Scilly that, along with St. Martin's, Bryher, St. Mary's, and St. Agnes, form the end of Cornwall. Islands with saints' names can only be paradisiacal, especially if one grows gardens there. The gardens are Mediterranean, of course, for the Gulf Stream passes close by, but the idea of a garden on an island is ever seductive. The image of the garden par excellence, that of Paradise, was it not one of an island? We owe this marvelous creation to August Hamburey. After having made a fortune, in 1834 he rented all the islands and began an exotic garden on Tresco. Helping sailors and founding schools, he was looked upon as a king. He abandoned the other islands in order to concentrate on Tresco, which he bought. Then, as in a fairy tale, four generations followed, each passionate for the gardens. The second generation rebuilt the walls and grew a better protection for the garden by planting on the north and east, for the winter winds can blow up to 100 miles per hour. The third highlighted the Mediterranean side, bringing in plants from Australia and South Africa. The fourth generation repaired the damages caused by snow in 1987, and in 1990 by the violent storm that felled eight hundred magnificent trees! Depressing? No, for here the earth is like cake, acid, siliceous, and light; everything continues to grow in winter. The Hambureys replanted sixty thousand trees, reinforcing the

ABOVE AND RIGHT: *Old
pots, eaten by salt
and mosses, are planted
with delicate flowers.*
BELOW: *In the heart
of a round rock grows an
Ombellifère.*
OPPOSITE: *In the foliage
of a* Brugmansia sanguinea
*from Brazil, a shower of
yellow and orange flowers
called Angel's Trumpets.*

screens, multiplying the species, and extending the gardens over the entire island. In 1983 they found a pearl in the person of Mike Nehams, from the Royal Horticultural School, Wisley, Merritswood College, Surrey, and Plimpton College in Sussex. Mike is an excellent botanist and has also worked in France and in Italy. He organizes tours in South Africa, Argentina, and Australia. He knows everyone. And, on Tresco, he goes so far as to greet visitors who arrive by helicopter in limited numbers.

The helicopter awaits us at Penzance, twenty-eight miles from Tresco; one arrives in ten minutes after having flown over a marbled sea that resembles Tinos marble, named for the Greek island, a brechoid green marble enlivened by white calcite veins.

The island seems to be divided up into a multitude of coves and beaches with turquoise water, and a wild air of surprising beauty. One lands on a perfect lawn, a true golf green punctuated by several white spots—seagulls who have come to rest on it. We approach a wooden house that serves as a reception hall, bordered by a little dry stone wall covered by mosses and bordered by ferns and *Agapanthus*. Such a wall immediately bears witness to the marvelous marriage of the mineral and vegetable here. We follow this wall along a road bordered on the other side by several palm trees, *Echium,* and masses of giant *Gunnera,* which

ABOVE: *The "flag garden,"*
inspired by the Union Jack,
is composed of white, pink,
and mauve tones.

convince you by their astonishing size that you are in an exotic foreign land. Enormous stone foundations, on which pivots a gate, constitute the entrance, beyond which one makes out magnificent palm trees, *Phoenix canariensis.*

The gate opens onto a mass of bamboos, underlined at their feet by ferns and close by a thirty-foot-high *Brugmansia,* from southeastern Brazil, which rains down tubular flowers in tones of yellow, orange, and red, nicknamed Angel's Trumpets. Enormous rocks, placed one on top of another, indicate the monumental side of the garden and recall the idea of Prince Pallagonia who had the tops of his palace walls carved with monsters to surprise ordinary mortals! The rear part of the castle is unveiled, constructed half of rocks, half of dressed stone. It is perched on a mountain of rocks, bristling with yuccas and tufts of bushes with gray-green leaves and pink flowers: *Euryops chrysanthemoides.* On the heights, the silhouette of an *Araucaria* appears against the sky like a shadow with its airy suspended forms that seem carved.

Our gaze is then drawn to the left by a gigantic trimmed wall of vegetation almost thirty feet high. Everything in this garden is constructed, carved, drawn, and structured, and at the same time the illusion of a disorderly multiplication is very strong: that is the signature of gardens in the Italian style.

Before this wall, one thinks of that of the cemetery of Forcalquier
and of all those spectacular walls of the most ancient gardens of Italy.
Dizzying, it immediately inspires the image of fantastic palaces and at
the same time of ruins. What's more, a path leads to a concealed door
that opens onto an enclosed garden. It is the garden of the abbey, which
is the oldest part of the island and whose ruins, in the rear, preserve several tombs in the middle of a flowering garden. Following the rising
path, one comes upon a mass of *Acacia verticillata* with very fine foliage
and covered in yellow blossoms. One could say it's dusted with colored
pigment! Along with several rocks it outlines a vaulted entrance from
which a forked path begins; one direction leads to the lower garden, the
other to the upper one. We take the upper path in order to find a high
point to survey the whole garden. Thirty-foot-high palm trees, *Phoenix
canariensis* and *Jubaea chilensis,* cap all the vegetation. Beneath one finds
other palm trees, the very tropical *Cordyline australis,* down to *Cycas,* and
Yucca gloriosa, with little white bells. The *Aloe arborescens* with red flowers are also abundant. Echiums, cypress, and junipers burst toward the
sky, the vegetation of the lower layers abundant and heavily in bloom. As
for the foliage, gray-greens predominate. The flowers here are blue,
notably *Agapanthus praecox orientalis* and beds of hyacinth blue *Scilla
peruviana.* Then the reds reassert themselves.

One is convinced that

this is an exotic foreign land.

ABOVE: Kunzea baxteri.
OPPOSITE: *A slope carpeted with flowers.*

Among the reds, the most spectacular are those of the *Metrosideros,* which are trees with smooth velvety brown trunks that sometimes grow to over fifty feet high. There are also the red flowers of the *Watsonia* from South Africa, the trumpetlike flowers of the *Lapageria* from Chile, the pompons of the Australian *Kunzea baxteri,* which flower in March and April, and the *Callistemon.* There are also dense bouquets of *Crassula* from Madagascar and Asia, up against the beds of *Gazania splendens,* a kind of daisy with gray-green foliage from South Africa.

In the yellows there are a multitude of acacias. There are also, with a very tropical appearance, *Aloe striatula,* which bloom from November to February, and the strange *Isoplexus sceptrum* in the form of snapdragons making a kind of scepter, grouped at the end of a stalk. There are mauves, too, in abundance, simple carpets of *Senecio* and *Osteospermum, Lampranthus, Scilla, Geranium maderense,* and the refined *Amaryllis belladona* (pink). These intense colors are the Mediterranean.

Advancing along the path one comes upon an old wall covered with moss, bordered with ferns at its base. This wall is overrun by white climbing roses as it descends toward the bottom of the garden. Not far from there, one discovers an oval pond covered with yellow water lilies, surrounded by lavender, *Santolina,* and agave. It is punctuated at the

four corners by cypress trees near magnificent palms *(Phoenix canarien-sis)* with trunks that resemble elephant feet.

Then one discovers the "flag garden," which is a tradition in Italy where families love to create a garden in the form of their coats-of-arms. Here the garden is in the shape of a cross forming the Union Jack with tones of white, pink, and mauve. But before reaching that point, we stop before the *Geranium maderense,* a disappearing species whose surreal hairy violet-red stalks make one think of Salvador Dali. The curiosities do not let up. On the nearby wall we discover a *Clianthus puniceus* from New Zealand with tullelike foliage as evanescent as that of the asparagus that keeps it company and with flowers shaped like commas, next to a *Lochroma fuchsioides* from the Andes, which has ravishing red "weeping" flowers. Nearby grows a splendid tree from Burma with long round leaves: *Daurauja subspinosa.* This garden is of such a botanical richness that it is enough to make one lose one's Latin! It is so luxuriant that one gets lost constantly, but wherever one finds oneself, it is always admirably planned and structured.

Arriving at the center, we find a staircase heading downhill that crosses the garden in a spectacular manner, giving it a spine right through. This drop is also found in all the great gardens of Italy. Seen

from below, it represents a climb toward the light from which all follows
symbolically. It also drops down to the sea, and it is this connection
between the fire of the sun and the water of the sea that controls everything. At the summit one is surprised by an alignment of majestic
Monterey cypresses from California that are 130 years old! From here
one overlooks the entire garden, making out the sea and the nearest
island, undoubtedly St. Agnes. Going down again by a staggered path,
one finds the Mediterranean garden: three terraces in stages with balus-
ters, ponds, cypress, olive trees, beds of white and mauve "daisies"
(Osteospermum), and centered on a pretty pavilion decorated with shells.

All the way at the bottom, almost losing oneself in the shady side
paths, one finds the recent extension of a garden. It remains exotic, but
this time in the English manner. Here grass paths are bordered by
Echium and Agapanthus under the cover of a tropical forest so that one
could believe that one was somewhere in the Indies or in Asia, in a
mythical English colony.

Coming back toward the abbey, off center but still in the heart of the
garden, one crosses paths covered by giant tropical ferns before arriving
at an entrance overgrown with vines and climbing roses that opens onto
the ruins of the priory of St. Nicholas. There a walled garden made of a

ABOVE: *The peaceful garden inside the ruins of the old abbey.*
OPPOSITE, LEFT: *A granite pedestal.*
OPPOSITE, RIGHT: *A wall covered with moss and flowers.*

bed of very simple flowers leads to the ogival entry to the abbey, which is overgrown with roses. One feels a great sense of quietude here. Bordering the entrance and mixed in with ferns, a *Fuchsia* drops its fine rain of little flowers. Rock roses from Portugal are planted everywhere. Near the gravestones grow heliotropes and borage with beautiful little white flowers. Peace reigns. The gigantic wall of vegetation that we noticed at the entrance to the garden borders the remains of the priory as if to ensure its permanence, troubled only by the arrival of the helicopter that has come to find us.

Confrontation
with Nature

Tom Armstrong is a passionate soul. In his personal and professional life he has always been involved with art and nature. He is considered one of the best directors that the Whitney Museum of American Art has ever had. Having been a director of four prestigious museums for more than twenty-eight years, we now find him confined to his island garden off the coast of Connecticut. Confined? You must be joking. Tom adores nature, the sea, and plants. "To have a garden by the sea is to accept confrontation with nature," he maintains. There he finds color and form and especially the ephemeral nature of things, which is the very characteristic of contemporary art. And as he also likes people, whom he cannot help but meet, he has been inspired by the celebrated Frank Cabot, founder of the Garden Conservancy.

"Frank Cabot has made us aware of the cultural heritage of gardens." The Conservancy's Open Days program provides access to more than four hundred private gardens in twenty-six states. They also organize weeklong visits to Arizona, Charleston, Seattle, and other centers of horticultural interest. "When I was young, my parents wanted me to be an architect, but having worked summers on a farm, which I loved, I wanted to be a farmer. I only lasted a year and a half at Cornell's college of agriculture before becoming disillusioned and returning to the study of fine arts. My wife's family came to this island from New

Opposite: *The shore is lined with rose bushes.*

I like playing with fields of colors.

ABOVE: *The round beds of the Japanese garden. In the middle, a rhododendron in full bloom.*
OPPOSITE: *A romantic corner of the garden in two different seasons.*

York when she was young, and so we brought our family here. We are forty-five minutes by boat from the mainland. We got in the habit of renting small houses like one would rent a mountain cabin. Since we entertained many friends, we finally bought a house and created a garden around it that goes down to the sea.

"The island was originally a large farm that had been given by George III to Governor Winthrop in the eighteenth century. During the First World War, it was a military base. All this has disappeared. There are no hotels, no restaurants, just a little grocery. One sole road, but five churches! People love to get married here. Hurricanes were the first gardeners, bringing seeds with the wind, then people planted a great deal as well." Tom recounts all this as he drives us back from the small airport where we landed on a minuscule runway bordering the water. We leave the winding road at a wooden electrical pole that marks the branching off of a dirt road leading to the house. The pole is capped by a nest, almost as big as a stork's, where, Tom tells us, an osprey has nested. "It is a bird that comes from South America, a beautiful bird of prey." Tom loves Audubon and the other animal and botanical artists of the eighteenth and early nineteenth centuries; he has an exceptional collection of eighteenth-century natural history prints. We follow a straight path, "the only straight path on the island," he tells us, laughing.

ABOVE: *The paths are lined with rooms of greenery.*
OPPOSITE, LEFT: *Bearded iris and broom are planted near the shore.*
OPPOSITE, RIGHT: *An arbor draped with wisteria and clematis, lined with borders of blue flowers.*

The landscape architect Morgan Wheelock designed the entrance and areas immediately surrounding the house. The gravel path crosses under the shade of large trees in what at first seems to be a large park. Before arriving, one notices on the right a lovely movement of undulating land with hummocks sprinkled with wild iris arranged haphazardly, creating a nice contrast with the perfect English-style lawn. Our gaze is then drawn to the other side by a dark rock rising in the middle of small paths that lose themselves on either side in masses of rhododendrons and pink and white azaleas. "It is my Japanese-style garden. I love to create, by pruning, rounded masses out of large areas of vegetation and to establish vanishing points by pruning trees in clouds." Creating volumes in space, making backgrounds, that is the architect's side emerging! "Undoubtedly, and I also like playing with fields of colors."

The path ends in the exact axis of the house in front of which is a rectangular gravel courtyard, harmoniously proportioned and framed in a very original manner. The entire charm of this entrance comes from the slightly raised terrace from which one enters the house and which is entirely planted with apple trees pruned in plateaus, which keeps up a lovely confusion between trimmed vegetation and architecture and gives this house the feeling of a house of the South, from Virginia or Louisiana. Under this natural, deliciously shaded canopy each tree trunk

is surrounded by a square of pebbles, which lends a contemporary note. The white windows of the rooms on the first floor all open onto this layer of tender green foliage, perfectly pruned, which is also a delight when the apple trees are in bloom. It is very pleasant when one is still on the threshold, in the shadows, to see the blue sea through the entry door on the other side of the house. Another terrace extends the house on the sea side. It is centered on an agreeably proportioned pool in which float water lilies. It is as round as an eye, the eye of contemplation. From here one's gaze covers a part of the very green garden, the craggy rocks of the shore, and the entire landscape facing Connecticut, lightly mist-covered. On the left, the lawn descends progressively toward the rocks, first stopped by a low wall covered with climbing *Hydrangea petiolaris,* before forming a pleasant recess under a circle of parasol pines where one can withdraw to enjoy the breeze. The other side of the house is not made of curves in the English manner but rather conceived with French rigor. Yew trees designed in large table form lead toward a path of about twenty admirably pruned linden trees that are punctuated on the house side by yews and boxwood in the form of cones, with *Pachysandra* flowering at their feet. In the middle of the path a bronze statue of a crane in a pool that is splashed by streams of water stands

out. The path continues with rooms of greenery, one after the other. The first is a semicircular arbor; the second a fold protected by masses, a "booth" where one can come to read, take tea, stretch out on chaise longues in the most complete tranquility like a lizard in the sun, with the sound of surf and seagulls in the background. On the sea side, these rooms open onto a path laid out as a promenade. Bordered with flowers, yet keeping its wild aspect, it snakes along the shoreline between the rocks. In this open zone between land and sea—where one senses the open sea that frees one from the oppressive gravity that one sometimes feels in the interior, and where in the wind and the movement of water one likes to feel the proximity of solid earth—Tom has had a wooden seat built in the form of a perch. It leans up against a tree and one climbs up into it on four rungs of a "ladder." It is here that Tom comes to dream, to reflect or think of nothing at all, letting himself be absorbed by the sound of the water.

The narrow path climbs up then down; it brushes against the water, then starts up again, bordered in spots by flowers that present them-selves like a discovery as they all have a wild air about them. There are astilbes, white daffodils, iris, of course (bearded, yellow, and the delicate dark blue japonica), and also columbines with little flowers. Maritime pines, several trees resembling acacias, honey locusts, and masses of bayberries make up the edge of the shore. A little cove forms the far end. It is completely virgin, and bordered on its sides by wild roses that make up true wildflower beds sprinkled with their pink, red, and white flowers with several spots of yellow. There is nothing more resilient and charming than these wild roses facing the sea!

Going back toward the house, we pass behind the arbor and take a grassy and shady path bordered by iris, butterfly bush, hosta, and masses of *Hydrangea*, which is well suited to this sheltered spot. There is *H. quercifolia* 'Tennessee Clone', whose panicled inflorescence appears as vigorous as it is delicate. The undulating sepals are pale white-green and the leaves, which are cut out like those of an oak, turn

BELOW: *Coming out of the Japanese-style garden, a wood bridge between tulips and ferns leads to the shore.*
OPPOSITE: *Sailboats glide by in the Sound.*

red in autumn. An *H. aspera sargentiana* accompanies it. The sargentiana, originally from China, is a bush of ten to twelve feet high with white flowers that blossom around fertile dome-shaped flowers, the purple flowers of which turn to mauve. Further on one finds *H. paniculata* 'Grandiflora', introduced from Japan by the celebrated botanist von Siebold. It creates a superb mass with marvelously delicate flowers, which at maturity are spotted with old rose and which resemble silks from a Louis XVI salon.

Nearby, the tennis court has been transformed into a garden of pots. It has been literally annexed: Passions are invasive. It is bordered by other hydrangeas, peonies, and dahlias. On a path punctuated by boxwood pruned into balls, one heads for a flower garden, surrounded by a

RIGHT: *The shell-paved lane.*

OPPOSITE: *A grass path, bordered by white agapanthus and pink rhododendron.*

A winding path permits

one to snake in and out.

hedge of 'New Dawn' roses that contains a collection of tulips. This is also a cutting garden to provide flowers for the house. One leaves this garden by a delightful tunnel of mauve *Wisteria* covered at its feet by *Clematis canadensia* like violets and blue *Agapanthus* in pots. The end of the tunnel opens onto the gigantic trunk of a maple tree, surrounded by masses of white rhododendrons.

From there a quiet winding path that is a like a golf green permits one to snake in and out in the English manner among the rhododendrons, weighted down by flowers, to end up in other rooms of vegetation. Along the way, one passes Japanese dogwood, masses of tree peonies that Tom adores, and variegated hosta, with prettily grouped lungwort. One ends up in a garden of greenery surrounded by a crown of maritime pines bordered by balls of boxwood and holly and centered on a shell-form fountain. A *Styrax obassia,* which is a tree with very light foliage, serves as a considerate parasol for a bench. This bench offers in perspective, from the end of another green path, a view of a circular pool in which a provocative Venus appears to fall.

We next arrive in a more open space, having passed under the foliage of a superb *Magnolia* before venturing into the Japanese-style garden. Here the paths snake off in all directions among the masses. The light, filtered by the foliage, is very soft. It moderates all colors. One is especially surprised to discover the richness of the greens. This filtered light holds everything it illuminates in stillness in such a way that one experiences a feeling of peace and at the same time a great pleasure in gazing upon each thing. Here the grass gives way to a carpet of moss. Several pink and white rhododendrons form thick masses. Conifers are pruned in cloud forms, creating very agreeable backgrounds and sight lines. A honeysuckle whose shape has been adapted only appears progressively as pruned into the form of a carp, as if things needed time to uncover themselves to you. Groups of ferns, with foliage as delicate as that of maple trees, are joined by *Gunnera,* hellebores, and white-flowered *Hosta.* One moves about in this space with both a sense of religious respect and immoderate pleasure.

We leave this bewitching spot by a path bordered by lilacs, astilbes, and *Rodgersia tabularis,* which gives the impression of being in a jungle, as well as ferns that come up to our waists. We then cross a little wooden bridge to reach an extraordinary path of shells, which break under our steps with a sound as delicate as the rustling of silk.

The golden, luminous mass of a *Berberis* 'Aurea' marks our departure from the shadows. We are now on a thick and very soft path of cedar bark, which silences our footsteps and leads us to the rocks of the shoreline near the house. Here we find Tom again, who, after we have thanked his very kind wife, accompanies us to the airport, inexhaustibly full of projects and wanting to show, after the governor's garden, the gardens of friends, so that we will undoubtedly have to take the next plane!

OPPOSITE: The French garden. In the foreground is a daffodil bed under the lime trees; beyond, a succession of cone-trimmed boxwoods.

A Tropical Garden at
the Edge of Etna

OPPOSITE: *A mass of exotic plants creates a tropical atmosphere.*

Facing Naples, on the island of Ischia, Lady Susanna Walton and her late husband, the composer Sir William Walton, created the most beautiful tropical garden in Italy. Yet when they began La Mortella, there was no road, no soil, no water, no electricity, only rocks swept by the wind! Susanna was born in Argentina where she met her composer husband, who had come from London to give a lecture at the English consulate. He carried her off with the idea of settling on Ischia. He needed sun and peace. But just after the war it was difficult to land on the island, where roads were rare, as was gasoline. Yet here they were, arriving in a Bentley. Either one is English or one is not. Finding a spot overlooking the sea, Susanna began to dream of gardens. Their friends, baffled by this crazy idea of creating a garden on the rocks, introduced them to Russell Page in hope of dissuading them. Alas, Page found the idea of a garden on wild rocks interesting, and all attempts at dissuasion were set aside before Susanna's temperament of granite and fire. And Page lavished his advice on them: It requires time, one must make several attempts at planting, and the plants must be young because the wind uproots trees that are too big. On the aesthetic side, he recommended removing all Ampelopsis vines in order to underline the dramatic aspect of the location. And as curves dominated, he advised developing straight lines, notably by making a pool from where a*

RIGHT: *Detail of a terra-cotta fountain.*
BELOW: *The house, surrounded by luxuriant vegetation, blends into the mountain.*
OPPOSITE: *A canal lined with mauve hydrangeas crosses the garden, giving it a definite structure.*

The most beautiful

tropical garden in Italy.

rectilinear canal joining several fountains would be like the vertebral column of the garden. Susanna, enthusiastic, got down to work.

Truckloads of earth were ordered, and Susanna had the fiendishly clever idea of having all the garbage from the area delivered there, to be transformed into compost. A large cistern to gather rainwater was installed. For protection from the wind, Susanna planted silver-gray cypress and oleander. Next she took trips around the island to gather bulbs and became an expert in cuttings. From Argentina she brought jacarandas, Judas trees, magnolias, chorisias, and red-flowered eucalyptus. But she also introduced into her garden ginger flowers with a delicate scent; Canary ferns; evergreen *Calliandra pulcherrima,* with red balls; camellias, which flower from October to April; and Mexican and Australian plants. In 1964 her husband did a world tour and sent her a great number of plants, such as *Metrosideros* and tree ferns, from the great botanical gardens. This was the beginning of their tropical garden, which a watering system of clouds of rain would make possible.

One enters into a garden whose luxuriant vegetation has overtaken the rocky hill. On the path, which winds as it goes up the hill toward the house built into the rocks, one first finds a collection of camellias, and on the other side of the path, a collection of spiny trees. One passes a

BELOW: *Looking down toward the sea. Pine and cypress trees remind us that in spite of the tropical plants we are still in Italy.* OPPOSITE: *Near the pavilion brought from Thailand, large* Colcasia *leaves sway softly on their elegant violet stems.*

Magnolia from China; with their very similar leaves, camellias and magnolias go beautifully together. A path forks to the left. It is bordered by a low wall prettily overrun with little ferns and disappears below into enormous masses of white and mauve hydrangeas. A *Magnolia grandiflora*, pruned into a pyramid, and whose branches are cut in a very airy fashion, crowns this descent. Still following the same rising path, one comes across a *Gingko*, at the foot of which bloom tufts of fragrant *Amaryllis belladonna* from South Africa, and among the *Erythrina*, one finds *E. crista-galli*, which is the national flower of Argentina. They are accompanied by daturas, whose orange-yellow flowers, turned toward the ground like mourners, are suspended over a carpet of little blue flowers of the plumbago family. A magnificent incense cedar, *Calocedrus*

decurrens, which resembles a California *Sequoia,* majestically covers a bed of *Woodwardia* ferns nicely accompanied by *Acanthus.*

The music of a fountain is heard below among the masses of hydrangeas and tropical ferns. Before approaching the belvedere, one passes beneath branches of lemon, grapefruit, and mandarin orange trees that are weighed down with fruit. A magnificent flowering lotus grows in a pot to mark the first step of the banister, covered with honeysuckle and *Solanum wendlandii* from Costa Rica, with little pale blue flowers. The staircase leads to a large aviary from which trail the cries of brightly colored exotic birds, which melodiously filter into this garden and accentuate its tropical allure.

Right next to the house, our gaze is drawn down to a large round

OVERLEAF: *The garden is a conservatory for tropical species, among them plants from Borneo and Guatemala.*

One listens for the croaking of frogs.

ABOVE: *Tropical ferns.*
OPPOSITE: *A jet of water from the basin reinforces the luxuriance of the garden.*

pool, at the heart of which are placed several rock outcrops from which a tall jet of water bursts forth amid yellow water lilies, tufts of papyrus, and giant *Gunnera* leaves. This body of water is the work of Russell Page. It is of a great simplicity, linking the landscape with its rocks and the exotic allure of the garden through the plants. Around the pool, on top of the rocks is a collection of palms, agaves, and aloes, which are like a wreath reinforcing its luxuriant tone. The water leaves the pool to feed two fountains below by a straight canal, crossing the entire garden and sinking progressively into the masses of mauve hydrangeas. This stream of running water is bordered by hostas with white and mauve flowers and little grasses as cool and frail as a fine rain.

Taking a path above the house that winds around the mountain, one arrives at a rock in the form of a pyramid that is the tomb of Lord Walton. It offers a splendid view of the sea and the nearby volcano. Here Walton's soul hovers over the garden and the landscape. Continuing up, one discovers with surprise at this height among the rocks, with the sky above one's head, a large pool from which a jet of water shoots forth on one side. It is bordered by *Cycas* and *Gunnera*, tufts of rosemary, lavender, *Artemisia*, *Pontederia*, blue sweet peas, and *Agapanthus*. Susanna has nicknamed it "El Nido." Perched in the sky, with its still waters strewn

RIGHT: *From up high,
the views in this corner of
paradise are splendid.*

with water lilies, it makes a very peaceful corner. In spite of the presence of a bronze crocodile that lies in wait on the edge under a crown of leaves of an *Encephalartos manikensis,* one feels a great tranquility here. Then, after having passed on the path that continues on amidst a host of astonishing plants such as *Colcasia, Hedychium gardnerianum,* or *Alocasia macrorrhiza,* one finds a pavilion that comes from the ancient capital of Thailand, Ayutthaya. A myriad of white and pink sweetbriers, *Rosa rubiginosa,* climb the nearby trees. This little temple overhangs a pool of still waters where *Nelumbo* lotuses float like clouds in the sky. European chain ferns *(Woodwardia radicans),* masses of papyrus, reeds create a rather wild border to the pool. Here one floats. In the sweetness of the air, while waiting for the end of the day, one listens for the first croakings of the frogs, which gradually burst forth and animate the greater part of the night in this garden that is their paradise.

A Botanical Garden
in Portugal

The European Community has recently classified this region of Portugal as a Natural Park. The Ria Formosa Park has thus become a bird and flower reserve. All this has delighted our friend, who, coming to Portugal several years ago, was so captivated by the spot that he quickly sought and found a vast property facing the ocean with a typical farm. He dreamed of creating a garden with the spirit of an organic garden, a garden of wild flowers and nourishing plants with no transgenic hybridization. As a child *he had had a little shed at the back of his parents' garden where he had his own corner where he could grow whatever he wanted. He had also been intrigued for a long time by a neighbor who carefully selected herbs in the old tradition of herbalists. In Berkeley, California, he discovered organic gardening, which he now seeks to crystallize here on this magnificent site.* "Of course, I don't *want it to look like a vegetable garden! With the Japanese architect Shigeru Ban, I have a project for five greenhouses: for local potted plants, for tropical plants, plants that grow in sand, those that grow by the sea, and nutritious, medicinal, and aromatic plants and flowers from Europe, Asia, North America, and Australia. Beginning with an Internet site, we are going to organize a virtual visit of the garden, a way of opening it to everyone and, at the same time, the only way to preserve it. Dominique Guillet, who runs* Terre des Semences, *has a tomato field with two hundred*

Fragrance plays its

role in this garden.

ABOVE: *A riot of orange.*
OPPOSITE: *The path leading toward the shore is bordered by fig and almond trees.*
OVERLEAF: *One view toward the sand bar and the sea.*

and fifty varieties in very different forms! I have worked with him and have already planted six hundred nutritional plants. When I arrived here, the trees were withering away. They were old almond and fig trees. I had them pruned by my old friend Robert Middleton, gardener at Kew Gardens, who also found groundwater and was able to save many dying trees. He said to me, 'During one year we are going to make tests to see what takes hold and what does not.'

"I have a rather important collection of pelargoniums because I realized that in South Africa they grow on the beach! I brought some back and planted them on the sandy slope. They took root and became bushes that need no water. It was the same thing for the collection of thymes, which Jekka McVicar takes care of. They make up a whole avenue facing the sea. One must observe and experiment in order to adapt."

Fragrance as well as shape play their roles in his garden. We, therefore, have a "fractal" garden here, which blends technological and virtual dimensions with botanical and artistic ones. It is made of collections in a thousand layers that are intertwined.

The road along the coast, bordered by native oleanders, passes by this botanical garden. The entry is planted with a dozen cypresses grouped like an honor guard. They mark a dirt road that forks off on one side toward a little wooden house weighed down by *Bougainvillea* and

surrounded by wild grasses. This gardener's shed makes one think of
the shed hidden in the middle of the countryside where Rousseau wrote
his *Confessions.* We follow the main road with an olive grove on one side
and a succession of fig trees on the other. It is bordered along its length
by masses of flowers in blues and pinks with a touch of white. There are
plumbagos, jacarandas, tufts of *Agapanthus,* echiums, hebes, and pink
statice. Before coming to the house, one passes a grove of wild acacias
from Australia with delicate foliage and covered with little yellow flowers, and casuarinas with foliage light as pine needles. Toward the house,
which one catches a glimpse of, a path wanders between masses of myrtle with red flowers, *Leptospermum* × *scoparium,* and palm trees. There is
sage, rosemary, santolina, and *Stachys lanata,* pink digitalis, pelargoniums, and, even more colorful, orange *Gaillardia* and yellow *Gazania* as
a ground cover. The big white house with little vertical openings is
crowned by a typical chimney. At the feet of a *Bougainvillea* that climbs
the house, two big terra-cotta pots overflow with white pelargoniums.
The low wall of the little terrace that borders it is also filled with a collection of pelargoniums in pots, many of which are fragrant. A path goes
around the house and crosses an undergrowth made up of *Catalpa*
'Tormentosa', callistemons with red flowers, and old almond trees.
One of them is entwined by beautiful blue flowers of the Pittosporaceae

147

RIGHT: *The fig tree path, lined with masses of pelargoniums, goes to the sea.*
OPPOSITE: *The garden becomes a festival of color.*

Encounters with the

sea are strikingly beautiful.

family, *Sollya heterophylla,* and by *Ceanothus.* In the same blues one also finds *Trachymene caerulea.* All these blues in the shade give a note of coolness. Under the catalpas, pink umbellifers and a veritable ballet of *Agapanthus* 'Purple Cloud' create a very cheerful atmosphere, joined by a collection of daylilies. They are orange, yellow, red, and red-orange with yellow flowers. Continuing, one comes upon a delightful pergola with brick arches covered with roses. Among the roses are *Rosa* 'Baron Girod de l'Ain' from Vilmorin and *Rosa* 'La Sharifa Asma' from Delbard. It is surrounded by lavender and several ancient almond trees. Wooden armchairs in amusing forms allow one to doze off in the shadows, sometimes in the company of blackbirds, surprised and furious at the presence of interlopers.

We return to the coast side, passing through a palm grove made of paths of flat pebbles in ocher-red, iron-bearing soil. The palm trees are countless, from the most common, like the Chinese palm or the *Phoenix canariensis,* to the most rare varieties.

From here, a long avenue, flanked by fig and almond trees and bordered by masses of pelargoniums, mostly in reds or blues, goes to the edge of the shore that it dominates. As one progresses, one is struck by the richness of species and the astonishing variety of their scents that the breeze lifts to our faces.

On the right, in front of the house and up to the seashore, an immense field is planted with white, pink, and red *Oenothera*, which start flowering in the beginning of June and continue all year without being watered. This field of wild flowers in which small palms are immersed is absolutely magnificent. When one arrives at the seafront, one finds at the foot of a sandy cliff a plantation of several hundred umbrella pine trees, which seen from above make an immense green layer that seems to float in the air up to the edge of the blue sea. The crest is punctuated by several maritime pines and fig trees and skirted by masses of *Lantana*, geraniums, and *Osteospermum*, as well as bouquets of *Centaurea* with gray-green foliage, along with *Lavandula pinnata* and *Artemisia*. One also crosses pink columbine, *Gaillardia*, and *Cosmos*. Under the shade of the fig trees grow masses of rosemary and *Euphorbia* and, again, bouquets of *Centaurea*.

This encounter with the immensity of the sea and this long, very narrow band of sand, stretching out for miles like a deserted island, in a landscape without dwellings except for the clock tower of the church of a minuscule fishing village, is strikingly beautiful.

We take the second avenue that leads to the house. It is so wide and straight that it is called the "landing strip." It is bordered by masses of

OPPOSITE: *The narrow*
sandbar stretches for miles.
Beyond the thistle in full
bloom are bushes of rugosa
roses.

Artemisia, sage, *Gaillardia,* and lavender but is also planted with a collection of thymes. A long pool in the exact axis of the avenue closes this. Olive trees border it on one side and it is sheltered at the end by pepper trees and white hibiscus. On a level below, masses of fragrant orange trees are mixed with numerous *Cycas revoluta.* All the flowers here are white. It is the final point in the festival of colors that this garden offers. There are dune pinks, petunias, lantanas, *Westringia fruticosa,* and slender *Digitalis purpurea* × *alba, Scabiosa caucasica* 'Perfecta Alba', tousled nicotianas, statice, *Aquilegia* 'Alaska' with sepals as light as poppies, and lavateras.

On the return path one weaves between echiums and sages, as light as flax flowers, but also delphiniums and mauve *Cosmos.* Of course, one cannot leave this very attractive garden without the desire to return as soon as Shigeru Ban's greenhouses are in place.

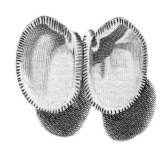

Palm Trees in Normandy

The Chateau de Vauville is located on the Cotentin peninsula of Normandy at the foot of wooded hills and fields sloping down to the sea. Here, the landscape and colors are very close to those of England, Ireland, or Scotland. The sky is often gray or pale blue, and the light, thanks to that, is always very gentle, which beautifully brings out the palette of greens: watery green, moss green, ivy green. But here is the surprise: Into this atmosphere of blended, slightly rusty tones come the bright colors of plants that one usually finds in the tropics. The Gulf Stream, which creates a microclimate hospitable to these unusual plants, explains the presence of palms, echiums, and astonishing giant gunneras, as well as enormous mimosas in bright yellow, red-yellow strelitzias, or the brilliant colors of tritonias. The owners, the landscape architect Guillaume Pellerin and Chloe de Turckheim, love this wild country made up of large spaces, which their chateau inhabits like an island lost in nature, and are garden fanatics. When one is standing on the shore, there is nothing more beautiful than to see the roofs of the towers, barely emerging from the mass of vegetation into which the chateau tends to blend, totally becoming one with the landscape.

In addition to the plants that are astonishing in their size and color, what is attractive here is this vegetation at the edge of the sea, bent over, protected, and in contrast to the open

ABOVE: *The bell tower rises behind a wall covered with ancient roses; at its feet are several bushes of white hydrangeas.*

OPPOSITE, TOP: *A perfect lawn sprawls under the tall pine trees.*

OPPOSITE, LEFT: *An arch covered with roses.*

OPPOSITE, RIGHT: *Bushes of gigantic gunneras.*

OVERLEAF: *One of the immense garden rooms.*

spaces, the receding hills and the ocean that one feels everywhere is close by. Here, nothing is closed in on itself but only protected, and this intimate side of this garden, composed of rooms of greenery, is pleasant just because of the immensity of the space. What is more attractive than to pass from a green room with a perfect lawn and masses of flowers as refined as a mixed border to the disheveled side of strong winds and tufts of grass and pines that have been bent by the gusts? Finally, the charm of the garden at Vauville comes from the well-ordered confusion between earth and water, through beds of lawn in the English style, so perfect that they resemble a sheet of water covered by duckweed and vice versa. Neither inside nor outside, but something in between; neither solid earth nor deep water, but a mixture of the two.

When one returns from long walks, whipped by the sea spray, deafened by the crashing of the waves to this beach of green, protected from the wind, one has the impression of entering a world of silence, calm, and mildness, a luxurious world where everything is perfectly cared for while appearing natural.

Trees and masses of vegetation surround the chateau, dissolving into the green and yellow masses of pines, palm trees, mimosas, and bushes of broom. As one gets nearer, at the end of a grassy avenue, the remains

of an old moat bordered by a very high wall, one finds the ancient granite chateau with its mullioned windows, its grayish roofs and its towers
before a large courtyard. It seems placed there for all eternity, as immov-
able as a rock. It has been there for such a long time that it is one with
the hills and the plants. It has, in some way, sunk into them. All these
old walls that frame courtyards and passages are beautifully in flower
with masses of hydrangeas, bunches of ferns and roses. Sometimes,
scattered in disorder as if they had reseeded themselves, a flood of deep
yellow narcissus spreads out over the lawn. When one raises one's head,
above the high protective walls, the big dark branches of California pines
stand out in a very airy manner. A big round tower, undoubtedly the former dovecote now fitted out, rises behind masses of reeds and white
hydrangeas. When one follows the road that winds through these
masses, one goes around the dovecote surrounded by pines, palm trees,
and giant echiums whose stalks point to the sky in a movement of aspi-
ration, and discovers a great grassy expanse that is a delight to the eye.
As the sun goes down, it is beautiful to watch the shadows of the echiums cast on the lawn. A single stone, rising up, has been set into this
expanse like a little island, a movement taken up by the palm trees in
the background that crop up from great masses of reeds. This lawn is

Charm here comes

from well–ordered confusion.

ABOVE: *At the feet of giant echiums, a mass of yellow Aloe stratula.*
OPPOSITE: *Under a beautiful Norfolk Island pine, a colorful floral composition reflects itself on the sleepy surface of the basin.*

bordered by giant gunneras that form a kind of low hedge. It lets one make out the sea and the cliffs in the distance, as a horizon line.

A path sinks into the flowering masses and one quickly has the impression of being lost in the middle of a field, but with flowers that submerge one everywhere. Then one finds a pool and crosses a wooden bridge that spans a waterway covered in duckweed. Here, the confusion between earth and water begins. One tends to take the grassy paths that snake in and out of the masses of vegetation or the expanses of lawn under the shadows for bodies of water covered by duckweed. Having passed by a palm grove—the garden has nine varieties of palms—one rejoins, through several masses of flowers, the path that leads to the sea, with the impression of open nature and the feeling of great liberty.

A Garden of Grasses in Rhode Island

OPPOSITE: *Close-up of a field of wild grasses.*

A wild property of fields and abandoned woods on the peninsula of Rhode Island overlooking the ocean, that is what was discovered by our solitary walker on a hike. Filled with wonder at this free nature, completely intact, he never ceased dreaming of saving this spot and creating a nest, one might say, without disturbing anything. More exactly, he sought to underscore its wild character, which, in a society where everything has become artificial, has become the ultimate luxury itself. In the United States, a reaction to the gigantism of the country, before the crushing and inhuman side of the Rocky Mountains, man has always harbored the desire to cut the land into manageable pieces. Look at towns and the ideal image of nature assimilated into a golf course with grass as far as the eye can see! At the same time, there has always been a love of wild open spaces. That the idea of liberty is associated with the natural philosophy of a Thoreau is not by chance, any more than the fashion nourished by the Rockefellers, among others, of "rustic camps." In our day, the understanding of ecosystems and Earth Art, forty years in advance of Europe, bears witness to these reunions of man with nature, of which this wild garden is, in its way, an expression. Therefore, in order to accomplish his desires, the owner called on a landscape architect from the University of Michigan, Lassus van Sweden, who is also a designer, that is to say, a landscape designer in the New

The garden bears witness

to the reunion of man with nature.

ABOVE: *A sober architec-
ture and an abundance
of flowers creates a sharp
contrast.*

OPPOSITE, TOP: *The boat
landing built of wood with
brass details.*

OPPOSITE, BOTTOM: *A
sunny carpet of rudbeckia
goes out toward the shore.*

OVERLEAF: *A wild sea of
grasses.*

Style movement. The landscape is to be treated in its entirety; instead of a garden that is merely a piece of the landscape, it is to be entirely merged with it. "This garden has nothing to do with the laying out of a garden around a weekend house, but it is the will to achieve a true communion with nature," says the owner. Thus, the landscape architect must first physically immerse himself in the location by wandering about it so often that he knows it by heart and assimilates it, if one may say, into his own body. Because, "in the beginning the space seemed so large that we did not know where to begin." It is the space that commands the geography; one thinks with one's body, never in the abstract. It was necessary to think about the mixture of forest, fields, and rocky coast and to translate this atmosphere of wildness full of charm. "It took me one year to clear the land in a selective manner, to define the outlines while distinguishing the special features, the faults, and the good qualities." One recognizes a piece of land by its contours and boundaries; isn't a country defined by its frontiers? Didn't the French philosopher Gilles Deleuze say with a certain degree of humor that "love is a question of surfaces," or the biologists claim that the beginning of life is but a question of skin, a gut reaction? Before closing itself up and becoming more complicated in the interior, a cell coincides with its surface; it is only surface contact.

168

"We finally found ancient walls of New England that we used to restructure the space even before construction of the house." The first landscape is a vast field, crossed from time to time by old dry stone walls. A large cedar gate begins a long winding path that ends at the house, which seems immersed in a sea of grasses where the presence of a redesigned wall can be taken for a "garden." As one approaches the sea, nature assumes its wild informal allure. One then crosses a second passage between walls that mark the entry into a forest of cedars where one already feels the salty breeze from the sea. Beyond these woods, the fields die out at the edge of the cliffs. One descends the cliffs by wooden steps one would think were constructed by sailors. Copper lamps placed on the jetties serve as lanterns.

As for plants, the colors are delightful. There are pale greens, dark greens, and gray-greens going toward yellows and reds and toward the mauves with delicate gradations and a touch of white from time to time.

The first field is made up of *Euphorbia robbiae,* lavender from Provence, *Veronica virginica, Perovskia, Echinops* 'Taplow Blue', *Caryopteris, Miscanthus sinensis* 'Rotsilber', and *Artemisia aborescens* 'Powis Castle'.

Near the house one finds heathers *(Calluna vulgaris),* alliums, and salvias. On the sea side there are artemisias and heathers, with *Calluna* 'Silver Knight', and lavenders, achilleas, veronicas, *Miscanthus,* and alchemillas.

Crossing the woods is magnificent with openings to the cliffs. One could imagine landscapes from Boccaccio. One reaches the cliffs by grass-lined paths. Sometimes a round rock emerges from the grass like the back of a whale in the ocean. Then one comes upon the cliffs made up of magnificent gray-black schist that peels off in places. It plunges into a calm, smooth, infinitely blue sea.

OPPOSITE, LEFT: *A mass of rudbeckia with a background of wild grasses.* OPPOSITE, RIGHT: *Grasses surge like vegetal fountains in the garden.*

Pleasure Gardens

A Garden in the Rocks

We had been visiting Corsica, and we embarked at Bonifaccio to reach Sardinia. The old citadel perched on a sheer rock that dominates the sea has the air of a fortified town with its narrow little streets that run down in a sheer drop to the port, situated between two cliffs, where the deep and transparent water is a surprising emerald green. Stationed on the back of the boat as it moves away, whipped by the air, one is captivated by the ink blue eddies crested by white foam in our wake, and one has the impression that the city is slowly melting into the rocks and ending up resembling a cave dweller's city, disappearing into the horizon. One quickly reaches Sardinia. The water is extraordinarily transparent but the landscape is different than in Corsica; the rocks are more rounded, with a more majestic scale. Taking the winding coast road that leads to the house, the rocks present an astonishing spectacle. Their shapes, monumental, cut up, and very suggestive, continually stimulate the imagination. Here one is on the edge of the Mediterranean, which is a blue as pure as the sky, at the same time in the desert and in the mountains. This is a powerful landscape, wild, raw, without concessions. We approach Porto Rotondo, surprised at not having discovered any ancient villages. This is because the Sardinian farmers rarely settled along the coast, seaside property having little value as pasture or farmland. Women were given

176

ABOVE AND OPPOSITE:
Pink laurels abound in the
garden.
RIGHT: *Water cascades*
from pink granite rocks into
the pool.
OVERLEAF: *Here one is on the*
edge of the Mediterranean.

The house itself is like a large rock.

these lots as dowries. Thus, it has been the women who have become rich with the recent development of tourism on the island.

A gate of olive branches leads us to the garden from which one can make out the house. "My father traveled a great deal. He spent his child-hood in Brittany and loved Greece, where we went each summer. Passing here on a boat, this wild coast of pink granite that reminded him of Brittany, he noticed a small fisherman's cottage that resembled a bit those in Greece. Captivated, he bought it and met the famous archi-tect Couelle, who remodeled the house, which had never been finished. My mother is Uruguayan, and as children we would go to Uruguay in the winter. My ancestor Juan Capuro, who was a shipowner and had settled there, had a passion for gardens. Purchasing land, around 1880 he imported from Japan a collection of rare species of trees and planted a forest of magnolias! As I love architecture and decoration, I held onto this house, which is also ideal for children and for entertaining friends. With my husband, I planted a garden. We installed a swimming pool between the pink granite rocks and the blue sea. We live on the rocks. We have lunch on them, using large stone tables. We live as close as possible to nature, very casually. These stone tables belonged to the shepherds who lived here. They also used stone benches to sit on, which we have fitted out with backs, around the tables. For contrast and for

179

RIGHT: *The cove has been claimed as a swimming pool; sunbathing, deep-sea fishing, and boating are on the program.*

OPPOSITE: *After the activities in the cove, one goes to the outside dining room for refreshment.*

comfort we put large white cushions on them. We built a landing so that
our friends could arrive by boat. In the evening the landing and the cove
are lit as if they were private pools. For that matter, the entire garden is
illuminated by torches. In this very natural and convivial garden, we
spend marvelous evenings having fun."

The house itself is built like a large inhabited rock. It is all pink, surrounded by a terrace that, on the side facing the sea, is on the same level
as the branches of the pink and white oleanders from which it emerges.
Their leaves wave in the wind like ocean swells. The walls of the terraces
are weighed down by *Bougainvillea*. Each room has its own path that
leads to the cove. One reaches the terraced roof by a narrow staircase
and one has a 360-degree view with the impression of actually touching
the sky and flying over the sea.

The garden entrance is made up of underbrush that evokes the
"sacred grove" of the Romans. It is made up of cork oaks under which
one lunches in the shade. Several groups of gardenias with an intoxicating scent planted nearby bring an air of freshness. On the side, a path
runs through the foliage, making a lovely gap that opens onto the back
of the house on grassy land almost like a golf course. It is in the form of
waves, broken by several masses of pine trees.

In the front of the house at the height of the terraces is a mass of pink and white oleanders through which built-up paths lead to the cove. There, the children enjoy flushing little turtles out of the bushes. On the side, a large lawn descends to the pool. "It allows me to go on foot from my room to the sea. In the morning when the sun begins to rise, it is delicious to walk on the grass still covered with dew." The swimming pool is kidney-shaped. Round rocks pour water into it from a fountain. The wind here moderates the heat. When one stretches out to dry off and rest, the noise of the fountain plunges one into a false somnolence, accompanied by the far-off sound of a passing boat or the closer cries of seagulls. When one swims in this pool, one has the illusion of being in the sea. The contrast is striking, but very agreeable, between the immense sea, sometimes agitated, the bright air, and the green, always calm, expanse of the lawn, the flowers, and the birds. On the horizon, next to two hills with gray-green and ocher tones, a large white cliff completely unreal rises up, dropping 240 feet into the blue of the sea. It takes on different colors according to the time of day. At sunset, it is old rose, as delicate as silk while the water turns toward violet. When the moon arrives, a moon that is magnificent here, it is a very soft chalky white.

From the landing one often swims in the sea, which serves as a second pool. Here, in the rocks, the impression of isolation is total. The rocks, which look like the furrowed skin of an old elephant, delight the children who spend hours jumping from one to another looking for pools of water. "When we dock our boat after long trips along the coast, we always feel great pleasure in returning to this garden, which is a haven of peace for all of us."

The Charm of Simplicity

In New York we met a talented creator of jewelry, Christopher Walling, an expert in pearls and a great lover of gardens. He knows well photographer Erica Lennard's pictures of gardens. With a mixture of discretion and an irrepressible urge, he finally confides: "I have a house and a little garden on Block Island. If you would like, come for two days. I will pick you up at your hotel tomorrow." We take off the next day from a small airport in a twin-engine plane. Christopher holds his dog in his arms, a very affectionate Jack Russell who never leaves his side. Here we are in the air. The sky is full of gray clouds with rich hues, which must not escape the eyes of Christopher, accustomed to examining pearls. We fly high over the sea, and it too takes on a rather cold metallic tone. It is flecked with whitecaps. In spite of the noise of the motors, conversation continues. "Early settlers built all the mortarless stone walls that resemble those in the Irish countryside. Through these walls, they remain present everywhere on the island, part of our soul. They seem to reflect the force, simplicity, and authenticity that characterize the island. It is tiny; there are only 865 inhabitants. Everyone knows each other. There is a community spirit. We feel like we are embarked on the same ship, physically linked, with a common love for the island. Now there are only two farms left that grow potatoes and corn. There are several sheep and horse raisers. And of course there is fishing:

lobsters, tuna, swordfish. We try to limit new houses in order to preserve the wild character."

As Christopher shows us the island, one realizes that he is still getting to know it, after sixteen years. For years he has devoted himself to its preservation. One has the impression that he is physically part of the island, that it is his own possession, a part of his life, his home port, a kind of root in the middle of the sea.

When one first catches sight of it, the island seems very small in the immensity of the sea. As one approaches, one has the impression that it is rather low, with ravishing cliffs, neither too steep nor too small, fringed in places by sandy beaches.

"The island has always been rather poor, contrary to others that have been spoiled by the presence of too many showy millionaires' mansions." We land with a crosswind daunting to neophyte pilots on a tiny runway with a single shed at the end that seems deserted. Our feet barely touch the ground when we are buffeted by the open sea air, transparent and pure as if washed by showers and already intoxicated by silence. Here raw nature seizes your body. Nothing stands between her and you.

We get into Christopher's old car that takes us across winding roads bordered by stone walls to his house. One might fancy oneself lost

somewhere in Scotland or Ireland, while one is less than an hour from
New York! We spy four houses, one of which is the only grocery at New
Harbor, one of only two "ports" on the island. Several sailboats are
moored, motionless amid the cries of seagulls and the regular clanging
of lines. Here time stands still. Nearby is the hotel-restaurant, very New
England–style in white clapboard with a cedar shake roof and a large
veranda where several lined-up armchairs undoubtedly await the arrival
of someone to doze off with a glass of whiskey in hand while contem-
plating the sea. The weather has now lifted and the sea and sky are pure
blue. All the houses are of the same style, painted white with gray wood-
shingled roofs softened by time, with a porch and always an American
flag planted in front! This unity has a great deal of character, linked as it
is to that of the wild landscape in its gray-greens, with the strong presence of sky and sea.

"For six years I lived in rented houses so that I could really know
the place where I would feel best. Ten years ago, I found a half-
demolished house on a dominant point of land that faced the sea and
was protected by vegetation." At the end of a dirt road lined with a hedge
of wild roses, we come upon a Y-shaped fork in the road, marked by two
stones set up as milestones. The rising road ends before two gray-
shingled fishermen's houses with little white windows. The base of one

BELOW: *Jack, Christopher's Jack Russell, takes his daily constitutional.*
OPPOSITE: *Two huge terra-cotta urns stand on top of a stairway surrounded by Spiraea.*

ABOVE: *Late afternoon may provide the ideal light for this perfect setting.*

of them is constructed from enormous stones that come from the clearing of the property's own fields. This monumental, earthy aspect stands in contrast to the small size of the house and accentuates its cabinlike charm. The two houses are surrounded by a forest of brushwood in red-greens with several openings to the blue-green sea. "I had the windows remade exactly with all their defects," confides Christopher, for whom imperfection is part of beauty. Is it not an imperfection in the oyster that creates a pearl?

Here one is at the end of the earth, cut off from everything, with the sound of the waves, the sea air that comes in bursts, and the peaceful forest, an ideal refuge for birds and rabbits. Here, in the immensity of the sea, one is sheltered. In this setting whose beauty is so wild, an artificial garden would have been completely inappropriate. The charm of Christopher's garden resides in its extreme simplicity and how it blends in with the landscape.

It consists, first of all, of a wide lawn bordered by a low stone wall that borders the brushwood forest. This lawn surrounded this way resembles still water. It seems like a pure green pool in a rude landscape, jostled by the elements—one might say the calm water of a port, free from the agitation of the high seas. Two great zinc balls, found in Nashville, Tennessee, that were formerly decorative elements of a monu-

mental portico tend to be confused with mooring posts on a wharf for the ocean liners on which Christopher frequently crossed the Atlantic as a child with his parents. "This garden of emptiness is my swimming pool," says Christopher. "I look at it and rest my spirit just as Zen meditation has taught me for the past two decades." This garden of emptiness, the only one I know that is not Japanese-style, is surprising early in the morning. From one of the bedrooms, even from bed, one has a view plunging downward, and like a dream at dawn, when the sun rises one sees, like a theater of shadows, the perfectly drawn silhouette of the house, progressively projected and moving across the lawn. This garden of shadows, very architectural, is unreal, like a dream. In the afternoon it is like a pool covered with pepper trees, touched by eternity while one senses all about one the rough sea. In the evening, at sunset, with its two monumental landmarks, it is imbued with the nostalgia of ports where large ships have come to dock or to leave forever.

On the other side, on another level, one finds the second garden that faces the front of the house. A big white porch, extending the house and partly covered by vines, overlooks a vast lawn with a curtain of lilacs at the end. They are white, pale mauve, and deep mauve topped off by a beautiful maple tree. Around the porch, partly made up of a trellis of natural branches, Christopher wanted a mixture of wild flowers and

ABOVE: *Elegant simplicity — a wood canopy made out of roughly trimmed trunks.*

OPPOSITE: *Outlined by an old stone wall, the orchard where a pear tree still stands.*

more refined flowers with a dominance of gray and white, always keeping a rustic side. At the feet of the climbing rose 'Sea Foam', which flowers from the beginning of June until mid-July, one finds white iris, several ferns, *Artemisia,* which reflowers in autumn if you cut it back in June, bouquets of *Dianthus,* which are pretty little white carnations, lamiums, astilbes, larkspur, and *Allium siculum bulgaricum.* Several cerastiums prolong the movement, with delicate little white flowers on gray foliage. As Christopher adores peonies, he could not resist planting several. White, they are a rapture of delicacy and purity. A bush of *Enkianthus chinensis* lends a note of yellow in May.

On the side of the house, two great jars, found in Atlanta, Georgia, frame a little staircase that leads down to a plot of land that slopes downward, covered by masses of pink and white *Spiraea.* They resist everything, seed themselves and proliferate. They seem at once wild and delicate, which is admirably appropriate here. One crosses these masses and plunges down lanes bordered by stones, to reach the port on foot or to take long walks on the beach. Here is the little paradise to which Christopher, leaving New York or returning from the four corners of the globe, comes to find himself again.

La Quinta do Muro

Along the road that takes us to La Quinta do Muro, one sees all over white houses that stand out from a soil that is a warm ocher, almost red, like iron-laden earth. And everywhere there are olive trees, umbrella pines, and cypress. Oleanders, which grow like weeds, border the road and let us glimpse at moments the sea, all blue. Arriving at a little intersection, we leave the main road for a prettily paved lane. Before reaching the house, it leads us at length across vineyards and then an olive plantation. Those trees along the road have their feet ringed by tufts of white iris. We come across large crates that seem to be destined for the harvest of olives and other fruit. In fact they are models of a land art project by Richard Serra. This road evokes the entry to the property of the prince in Visconti's celebrated film The Leopard. *At the very end we make out horizontal lines of white columns rising against the sky. The gravel inner courtyard, surrounded by a white wall, is punctuated on both sides by two old pomegranate trees, the symmetry of which reinforces the planned appearance of this place. A colonnade links the two parts of the dwelling and frames the viewpoint of the ocean in the background. On the large esplanade that extends the courtyard, two pools, the first of which is square and slightly elevated, create an effect of receding perspective toward the Atlantic. Here the architecture of Pierre Louis Faloci is*

ABOVE: *The inside garden,*
with its magnificent square
beds planted in a willful
tangle.
OPPOSITE: *An overall view*
of the inside garden and its
rigid geometry. The straight
line of a basin crosses the
garden on one side.
OVERLEAF: *Siesta — a*
hammock hangs between
two carob trees with a full
view of the coastline.

thought to give structure to everything. There is no viewpoint that it
does not frame. Across this play of colonnades, it has the effect of a
screen. But the staggering of these, notably in relation to the façade, creates an effect of great lightness. By a game of contrast, it brings out the
wild side of the landscape or the air of abundance of the garden.

The courtyard is very lively, like all true entries. The dogs of the farm
occupy it. They all bark each time someone arrives; the crunching of
footsteps on the gravel sets off the alarm! In the evening they spread out
on the terrace that extends the courtyard at the foot of the columns. This
colonnade has a strong presence, like that of trees. In the evening the
sun throws striped shadows on the paving stones of the path, which
seems to increase them. What is next striking is the power of this architectural grid, its clean geometric layout, the whiteness of which contrasts
with the pure blue of the ocean and the sky. There is a tonality both
Atlantic and Indian, an air of the high seas, and a nostalgia that one
finds in the poetry of someone like Pesoa.

Advancing along the esplanade toward the sea, one overlooks a cliff
from which one discovers a long lagoon that empties and fills up again
with the rhythm of the tides. A long and narrow dune separates it from
the water. Several carob trees (traditional in southern Portugal) on the
edge of the cliff stand out in dark silhouette. Two of them, close

198

together, have permitted a hammock to be hung, where it is delightful to spend hours reading and dreaming, with, as background noise, the prancing waves and puffs of iodized air, which intoxicate you, mixed with the scent of lavender, planted in an immense parterre up to the house. In order to preserve this magnificent landscape and its wild nature, the owners have developed this lavender garden, which almost resembles a field, but which in fact assembles a collection of all the species of these plants—mixed with wild thyme, rosemary, rosa rugosa, and lined by a collection of pelargonium—between the beds of which one can easily glide. This makes a kind of labyrinth, the colors of which are delightful, fading from dark blues to mauves, to light blues, to purples and white. The garden contrasts nicely with the architectural grid of the façade that makes one think of a kind of protective trellis, before the immensity of the ocean. During construction of the house in 1985 a tree was planted in the summer dining room. Its integration with the architecture resembles a work of earth art. Marriages of mineral with vegetation, this is what affirms this house in the heart of the landscape.

To reach the beach, one passes by the pools again. One then crosses a simple little garden made of South African lavender, salvia, rosemary, and thyme bushes. It has an arched gateway cut into the pittosporum that opens onto a large field, a field of wild grass and fig trees overlook-

The architecture

gives structure to the space.

ABOVE: *Water channels between the entrance courtyard and the garden.* OPPOSITE: *A sensational colonnade shows the architect's will to frame the landscape.*

ing the sea. On the side, a little staircase made of simple stones winds about descending the cliff, bordered by gorse, a mimosa tree, rosa rugosa, and cactus. Arriving at the foot of the cliff one passes a plantation of carob trees before reaching the beach. Pedal boats allow one to cross the arm of the sea. A quick and carefree crossing but also moving when, in the middle of the lagoon, one discovers this house whose very contemporary architecture contrasts strikingly with its environment of completely wild nature. When one lands on the dunes, a boardwalk like a suspended bridge allows one to reach the seaside. One then has the feeling of being on an island, cut off from everything, exquisitely alone!

Returning from our expedition, we enter the inner garden following the path of columns. At the end we discover a garden that has a closed feeling, being bordered on two sides by the house and crossed in its length by an ornamental pond. A classical approach, this design was originally found in Persia, then in India (at the Taj Mahal, for example), and in Hispano-Moorish gardens. But here, instead of being central, the pool is shifted to one side. Finally, it is crossed almost at its end by a narrow waterway that feeds a small semicircular pool, located on one side of the garden. Not very deep but nicely paved, bordered by tufts of water iris and pampas grass, it was conceived of as a watering hole for

202

the dogs and horses. Because of these shifts, this part of the garden has
a contemporary feel that fits in well with the architecture. The lawn is
broken up by sixteen squares of flowers that take up the architectural
grid. Nothing here is stiff or cold. Climbing plants attack the walls, and
the abundance of flowers in the squares balances with a lovely contrast
the geometric rigor of the whole. In this garden the unity of colors is
delightful, with only blues, pinks, and white. In the terra-cotta pots that
punctuate the colonnade along the bedrooms, *Plumbago* sets the tone,
then the *Wisteria* that climbs the walls up to the gangway leading to
the children's rooms. A collection of pelargoniums, pansies, violets,
sage, and heliotropes spreads out in the squares. Bordering the walls,
one finds blue and white iris along with roses. The large wall opposite is
covered with white *Bougainvillea*. This garden is a marriage between a
rather Mediterranean layout and squares of flowers that take up the idea
of an English mixed border while totally reinterpreting it. One could
say that the geometric rigor is only there to better emphasize the overwhelming profusion of flowers. It is a garden with a classical line that is
nonetheless contemporary. It has a closed feeling but the water breaks
the enclosure: The long, narrow pond ends at an opening in the squares
of the vegetable garden. Similarly, the second line of water ends at the

ABOVE: *The half-moon basin situated in the inside garden creates a rupture in its straight lines. Three windows open the space to the fig tree field.*
OPPOSITE: *The house stands in the landscape like modern sculpture.*

demilune pool set back from the wall and opens the view toward the fruit garden. The vegetable and herb garden, made up of a dozen squares of eggplants, beets, broccoli, lettuces, watermelons, pumpkins, and cutting flowers, is partially open to the orchard, which is laid out in long rectangles, the ocher earth of which, planted with orange, apricot, persimmon, quince, medlar, and peach trees, offers a pretty contrast with the lawn. The whole opens onto an olive and almond grove.

At the other end, the pond ends at a room of intimate proportions that opens onto two salons. From there, one's gaze crosses the house and discovers a view of the ocean. The room, bordered by stone benches, is centered on a ceramic table with *azulejos* made by Pierre Alechinsky. It is here that one pauses when the sun is too strong. Sheltered, surrounded by fragrant jasmine, one listens to the concert given by hundreds of frogs, and one feels through their song the breathing of this Portuguese earth, muffled, ocher, warm, and imbued with poetry.

A Garden of Sand
in Tunisia

OPPOSITE: *On the beach, Roman ruins mark the boundary between the ocean and the garden.*

Nothing is more naked than sand swept by waves that have drawn back. But those that return with the backwash bring a profusion of gravel, shells, bits of wood and seaweed to be carried off and reappear once more. Fascinated by this movement of water, one dreams of living on the beach. Enlivened by the sweep of the backwash and endlessly attracted by these objects deposited on the sand, one seeks, discovers, imagines. This game brings such pleasure that whoever has enjoyed it has trouble breaking away. This pleasure has no equal but that brought by gardens. For this reason, the person who loves the seaside is often the same one who loves gardens. To make things grow where there was nothing *before, to watch the trees that one has planted evolve, and the flowers one has sown bloom then fade and be reborn with the rhythm of the seasons, is to be at one with the flow of nature. It is to accept the passing time and to play with it. It is to know how to create true pleasure in living from the ephemeral dimension of things and at the same time to show a pronounced taste for beauty, which is the essence of the ephemeral.* This pleasure in *experiencing the passage of time and in cultivating beauty was that in which James Hensson dwelt. An American born in the Appalachians, he learned from several Cherokees the meaning of liberty and open space. He dreamed of nothing more, in order to escape the conditioning of society and to find happiness, than to*

ABOVE: *One discovers a
small temple standing
at the end of a long basin
covered with water lilies.*
OPPOSITE: *Majestic pea-
cocks wander in the garden.*

discover a corner of the Mediterranean on the seaside where he could
make a garden. A friend advised him to buy a large piece of land by the
sea in Tunisia rather than to go to popular spots like Capri. He fell in
love with a vast wild expanse of great beauty on the Gulf of Hammamet.
He quickly enriched the sterile sand with compost and replaced the salt-
water with freshwater from a spring that was found by a water-finder
brought all the way from Italy. It was in this way that this irresistibly
charming garden along the beach was born. Hensson built his house
here and put an irrigation pool in the garden. Then he drew the axes
that he wanted covered by shade and planted with cypress, palm, eucalyptus, and orange trees in abundance. Like the Romans of antiquity
who built their villas on this coast, he salvaged numerous columns and
stones to decorate his garden.

One day, Leila Manchari, who as a child had passed all her days running on these beaches, entered this garden like one who ventures onto
an island and discovered, astonished, plants that she had never seen
before. Surprised in her excursion by the watchdog, who frightened her,
she had the impression of being saved by the calming gesture of the
master of the property, whom she found as beautiful as a god, for the
child had never before seen a man with blue eyes! James Hensson
invited her to return whenever she wanted and called her Lily.

"I came here undisturbed and amused myself for hours. I made wreaths, I was alone; it was my world. I always felt great sadness when I returned to Tunis for school and to march in time. I decided that they would not get the best of me, that if I didn't want to 'die,' I would have to find myself. I knew when I returned to this garden that I had found this other world that I had been missing. I found the air of liberty at Hensson's place where he surrounded himself with his artist friends: Cocteau, Giacometti, or Man Ray and Paul Hortes, who had a house nearby. Like the taste he had for art and beauty, the gardens were proof that one could live for pleasure. It was at that moment that I decided to study at the Beaux-Arts in Paris. Later, Hensson fell ill. I took care of him for a long time. He died and, according to his dearest wish, was buried in his garden."

The garden turns toward the sea and extends up to the beach. It is surrounded by a high white wall, which protects it from the bustle of the town. Once over the porch, the noises of the city fade away and one feels far from everything in a place that has its own breath and lives for itself, outside of time, in an atmosphere like that of ruins or a monastery plunged into silence. One has hardly left the shadows of the porch when one is surprised by the luxuriance of the vegetation and the nonchalance of this garden whose charm is in its naturalness. A wide path of sandy

One feels far from everything.

ABOVE: *Delicate sand lilies.*
OPPOSITE: *A pool filled with spring water is a wonderful experience after swimming in the sea.*
OVERLEAF: *This pool, created out of Roman stones and columns, is filled with blue Egyptian water lilies and punctuated by high stems of papyrus.*

ocher soil, set off by a white border, gives the effect of a cut in an impressive profusion of majestic palm, olive, orange, oleander, and *Acacia* trees that grow without any preconceived order. As for colors, one thinks of Matisse with the whitewashed walls, the greens of the foliage, and the pure blue sky. In this garden there will always be the charming contrast between the perfect rectilinear plan of the paths, which gives the effect of a clipped and architectural space, and the disorderly abundance of vegetation. Advancing silently along the sandy path, one has a kind of unreal impression of traveling without movement. One passes by olive trees that are more than two hundred years old. Here, time is nothing but a worry; one no longer runs behind it.

Having emitted a cry that is at once strident and plaintive, a peacock crosses the path in front of us with such measured steps that it seems like an apparition! At the end of the path one finds a pool perpendicular to it in the shadows, full of water lilies. The noise of rushing water becomes more and more intense. It comes from a spring that feeds, in great floods, a completely white pool that is raised like a terrace and which supplies the whole garden. It is a pool that has a very ancient and contemporary look at the same time. Completely white, its waters reflect the pure blue sky; a square column emerges from its center. Leila comes to bathe in this deliciously fresh water after having swum for a long time

in the sea. The path, bordered by large trees that shade it, leads to the house. It offers a spectacular view. It is called the blue point, for one can make out far away, all the way at the end, under the branches that create the effect of a tunnel, the blue of the sea. The very gentle light, filtered by the foliage, casts leopard spots on the ground. Hundreds of *Acanthus* cover the undergrowth with their beautiful flowers, which recall the marvelous engravings of Gustave Doré illustrating Dante's *Paradise*. One arrives at the house, which opens onto a large rectangular courtyard. It is framed by olive and cypress trees at the feet of which are capitals from Roman columns, antique stones, and terra-cotta pots arranged in a haphazard manner. They are there like presents consecrating the longevity of the trees. The white façade of the house is formed along its length by a canopy made of columns that support arches covered with *Bougainvillea*. Wide steps, which unroll like a carpet, invite us to penetrate the interior patio where one finds, through the old stone and plants present everywhere, an atmosphere of peace and coolness. The *Bougainvillea* vines trace a framework against the sky. They resemble the drawings of Houtin.

Under the canopy, as evening falls, until night advances, numerous armchairs permit one to sit and doze and to pass delicious hours in the gentleness of the air, to talk or dream, by the light of lanterns, lulled by

the croaking of frogs. For on the axis of the house is a long pool strewn with water lilies and punctuated by a little temple at the end. Topped by a dome and whitewashed, almost lost in the foliage, it has a very Indian air. When darkness falls, the temple is the last luminous point in the half-light. A pergola made up of columns and covered with *Bougainvillea* and *Bignonia,* allows one to take a walk in the afternoon, protected from the scorching heat. A baobab, with its enormous force, has dislodged several columns. A little further on, in the shade, the ground is laid out in squares planted with white dahlias, giant zinnias, and fragrant pink "Belladonna" lilies. The entry to the path that leads to the sea is marked by an oleander with a delicious scent of cinnamon. A large stone rising up centers the end of the path. It is like a monumental sculpture that asserts the existence of the garden facing the sea. There one discovers a beautiful pool made of stones salvaged from Roman ruins. It is covered with blue Egyptian water lilies and centered on several papyrus with delicate foliage. The contrast is marked between the immensity of the blue sea, over which we have a bird's-eye view, and these still waters strewn with delicate flowers. Here one truly has the impression of being sent back to antiquity. A staircase, prettily punctuated by trunks of palm trees whose curves evoke those of a body, leads down to a white door open to the beach. On the sand grow very refined white lilies, which are called sea lilies here. The sea is thirty feet away. The temperature is delicious and the view is majestic.

Returning, one discovers a field of large cacti that seem like a group of people. Undoubtedly, without this wild spot, the garden would lose its natural aspect and a part of its charm.

Taking a path across the field, one comes to a design in the form of the sun, whose rays are punctuated by enormous palm trees. Nearby, under the branches, one finds the tombs of Hensson and his wife. That of James is an ancient Punic tomb decorated with shells. They are like islands in impeccably raked sand.

As it is necessary to save a bit of mystery in order to preserve the charm, we will not push any further the description of this great garden, which conceals numerous successive fountains in the shadows. We leave and rejoin Leila on the terrace surrounding the rear of the house to talk about plants and flowers.

Opposite: *In the shade of the palm trees, a shell horn of plenty is filled with cactus.*

A Virgin Island in Saint-Tropez

In summertime, the density of people in Saint-Tropez beats all world records! What is more, there is no invader more dreaded than Homo touristicus. But isn't the genius of man his ability to turn the bad into something better, to turn a constraint into a new liberty? That is to say, to succeed in a space that is saturated and asphyxiating in re-creating emptiness, in creating views, openings, and escapes that permit one to breathe again. And this garden is an escape. It allows one to dream, to nourish the illusion, understood as the true nature of reality—the illusion of wild nature, of solitude, of a space of peace and total liberty.

This is what the master of the property has accomplished, undoubtedly because he is of Lebanese origin and lives as if in exile, that is to say, always searching for an elsewhere from which he draws on the capacity to elevate this space and to make, here and now, a little Paradise. Here, that which is limited finds its conjunction with that which is unlimited; that which is enclosed opens always onto vast horizons. And what is interesting is neither the limited space itself nor the great horizons, but their conjunction, the incessant play from one to the other. That is one of the characteristics of this garden. The house, a large horizontal house, open to the sea by bays, overlooks a vast sloping plot of land that descends gently to the shore. It dominates the gulf over which it offers a majestic view with the Alps in the background

OPPOSITE: *A perfect lawn, lined with Cycas and flower bushes, calls to mind an expanse of sleeping water.*

216

ABOVE: *A view of the palm grove and the bay.*

ABOVE RIGHT: *The charming pool created by Niki de St. Phalle for the garden.*

OPPOSITE: *An agapanthus border protected by a hedge of tamarisk.*

OVERLEAF: *An infinity pool, which fits perfectly into the Mediterranean landscape.*

defining the sky and the sea, which often tend to become confused in the mists. This garden, abundantly planted with palms, cypress trees, and umbrella pines, whose airy silhouettes stand out on the horizon, this garden with the flat and smooth sea, almost infinite as background, gives the image of nature as heaven. On the crest, a sprinkling of pale blue *Agapanthus,* which joins the horizon line, gives the impression that the garden extends without limits, that it floats in the sky, above the waters, as vast as the view that it offers. The opposite slope is marvelously used to spread out large twisting avenues, edged with a perfect lawn, avenues that lose themselves in a network and curve beautifully among the palms and pines. The first avenue that goes downward is punctuated by a series of *Cycas,* which accompany the first steps. At their feet, white pansies underline their smooth dark green branches. Further on, a disheveled clump of lavender contrasts with masses of gray-green rosemary clipped into balls, which border the avenue. Continuing our descent, a large lawn appears behind bushes of white oleander, contained by protective hedges that give it the appearance of a clearing in the woods, or perhaps a little island, a bit like those few rocks that emerge solitary from the sea on the right. Wandering among the palm trees, one finally notices an even larger green room, at the end of which a magnificent wooden pavilion holds pride of place, covered by a

What is interesting is the

play of horizons and limited space.

roof in the form of a dome with a very Mediterranean appearance. Nearby, several trees clipped into balls are a lovely reminder of this dome, a reminder that blends nature and architecture. Several little palms decorate, on each side, the steps of this pavilion, which invite one to mount. Here the gulf is completely exposed, while one still overlooks the garden. The pleasure is to be at the same time on the sea and in the garden. One is practically on the shore and it is a delight to come here to dine, surrounded by friends, to take advantage of these long evenings with the presence of the moon on the waves and the gentle sound of the surf mixing with late conversations. At the edge of the shore, a curtain of tamarisks offers protection against salty winds, but it also, with its delicate foliage, gives the effect of a light veil that lets the blue of the sea appear transparently. Sometimes, several gaps of deep blue appear, as through a porthole. They are beautiful against the green ground.

From several spots on the shore this effect of different points of view onto the shore is reproduced, either delicately veiled by the light foliage or across this "railing" created by the pruned trunks of the shrubs. This gives a very agreeable atmosphere of intimacy, preferable to a sudden and brutal opening to the sea. In addition, these "windows" give additional depth to the garden. Some of the bushes, with carefully pruned trunks, extend this same impression into the interior.

ABOVE: *The sea seen through the soft screen of the tamarisks.*
OPPOSITE, TOP: *An exotic pavilion surrounded by palm trees.*
OPPOSITE, BOTTOM: *The shape of the nearby pavilion has sent the gardener into a frenzy of pruning.*

A little staircase with rounded steps makes a path through *Cycas* and masses of other vegetation. In the blue sky, several dappled clouds with grays like a van der Meulen take up this full form as do the pines, which have been clipped into rounded shapes. They lead to the marvelous swimming pool by Niki de St. Phalle, joyously colored and in plump forms. This original pool gives one the same happiness as that of water in a palm grove. Carmine red *Bougainvillea,* leaning toward violet, climb the palm trees; and white *Hibiscus,* with hearts spotted with red, respond to the colorful note of the pool. Around a bend, one reaches the shore bordered by another swimming pool completely open to the horizon, its waters becoming confused with those of the sea. A waterfall makes an agreeable sound when, stretched out in the sun, with not a thought in one's head, one rests here peacefully.

A Wild Garden in Malibu

Robert Dornhelm, an Austrian film director, and his wife, Lynn Osborne, a native of California, decided to build their house on this Malibu hill overlooking the Pacific Ocean. The very protected site has a half-wild air that Robert, who is passionate about gardens, decided to make into a garden integrated into the landscape once the house was built. 🌱 The couple's house is a large white structure built on the heights to get the greatest profit from the majestic view formed by the hills that slope down to the water. Up to the horizon, one sees only a succession of these hills that plunge into the sea. In the morning, everything is green, the ocean is very blue, and the sky is clear. In the evening, as the garden is oriented toward the setting sun, the gentle filtered light makes different greens stand out. The hill in the foreground is light green and then becomes darker before finally dissolving into a kind of luminous golden haze. 🌱 As nothing is more agreeable in order to look out over the landscape and dream than to be perched, our two friends made one of the roofs of the house into a terrace. There, between sea and sky, they have found perfect peace. The floor of the terrace has been deliberately left untended so that grass grows between the stones and everything doesn't give the impression of being clean and new. The wooden furniture is extremely simple. There is nothing at all affected here, for their only desire is to be in direct contact with nature.

Near the house they have installed a little swimming pool bordered by several palm trees and masses of yuccas—nothing Hollywood, only the will to enjoy the pleasure of bathing, overlooking the sea, with the impression of being on a mountain.

A Buddha holds court in the shade of a climbing rose that is situated next to the house, the canopy of which is scaled by a mauve *Wisteria*. There are even several hens, cherished by Lynn and Robert, who allow them excursions on the lawn!

Robert has planted numerous fruit trees: orange and lemon trees, which are fragrant in the springtime, plum and cherry trees. He sent for plants from Australia and Asia, exotic herbs and even vegetables. On the side of the hills, he thus made little wild gardens. A staircase sparely built from pieces of wood gives one access. It is bordered by cacti and agaves. Sprinkled on the slopes, one sometimes finds tufts of flowers that seem to grow naturally and which have a great deal of charm against this wild side. Of course our two friends enjoy escapades on these slopes, where they sometimes spend entire afternoons and which they also cross in order to reach the sea. Once one gets to know this garden dissolving into the landscape, one is obliged to recognize that the Kodak image of Malibu-Hollywood is no longer completely in fashion.

A Garden Above Big Sur

OPPOSITE: *Lupines mix their mauve flowers and gray-green leaves against a background of sky-blue sea.*

This section of the Pacific coastline is one of the most beautiful in the world. It has been admirably preserved by a nature protection organization that requires that each house—and they are very few—cannot be seen from the sea nor from the road. The cinematographer Vilmos Zsigmond, who has won two Academy Awards, and his wife, Susan Roether, a writer, have had the luck to be able to build a house with one of the most beautiful views of the coast, which was what Vilmos, who is a lover of light, sought, notably at sunset. ❧ He succeeded in finding an abandoned barn, which they transformed into a refuge. Susan, with the aid of botanical gardeners, created all around it a garden whose beauty lies in its extraordinary integration with the site. As the climactic conditions are harsh—strong winds, dryness, and storms—plants were used that were native to the locale and thus well adapted.

❧ One leaves the sinuous coast road to take a little road climbing under the pines and paved with broken stone sufficiently spaced to leave a large band of tender green succulents spotted with little purple flowers in the center. Having crossed these shadows, a beautiful vista offering a spectacular view of the steep cliffs and the sea appears through an opening in the foliage. On one side, a wooden deck, resembling a perch, overlooks the cliffs. At the foot of this deck and overhanging the sheer cliffs is a round pool made of large stones, the overflowing water of which

ABOVE: *From the house, a spectacular view of the coastline.*
RIGHT: *Lupines cling to the hillside.*
OPPOSITE, LEFT: *A rustic halt under the shade.*
OPPOSITE, RIGHT: *A splash of acid yellow.*
OPPOSITE, BOTTOM: *The dream Jacuzzi, its outside lined with stone.*

ABOVE: *On the rudimentary path, one takes a few steps down to the shade of pine trees.*

OPPOSITE: *The owners have created a haven where one enjoys the pleasures of the garden and the sea.*

reflects the sky before the blue expanse of the sea. Between two posts, a bench of great simplicity and sobriety has been built where one can admire the coast while chatting with the person who is bathing.

Several flat stones placed on the ground form a rudimentary path that allows one to reach the other part of the garden which is made up of a large rectangle of lawn, surrounded by pines and bordered by several masses of rock flowers. From here the view of the other part of the coast is marvelous, with the immense sea of deep blue, the coast hemmed by the white foam of the waves, and the succession of dark green hills plunging into the sea, which drown in the mists.

From the rear of the house, one descends by a path of round pebbles, bordered by pieces of stone, leading into the underbrush. Beautiful groups of rock flowers accompany each step. There are numerous succulents and different species of *Aeonium*. A big table of large planks with very simple benches permits one, in the shadows, in a filtered light that traces luminous patches everywhere, to eat lunch and draw tarot cards!

Vilmos rarely misses the sunset, which is like a ritual for him. In the evening the air is calm and gentle, the sea is peaceful and is now a warm gray-blue, while the setting sun washes the whole place with a rosy glow and the cliffs appear as a border of ocher-red.

Gardens to Visit

A very few of the special gardens in this book are open to the public.

Trebah Garden Trust
(Trebah, page 94)
Mawnan Smith
NR. Falmouth
Cornwall TR 115JZ
England
tel: 00 44 (0) 13 26 250 448

Tresco
(An Exotic Garden, page 106)
Valhalla
Tresco, I.O.S.
England
tel: 00 44 (0) 17 204 241 05

La Mortella
(A Tropical Garden at the Edge of Etna, page 132)
Via E. Calise 35, 80075 Forio
Isola d'Ischia (NA)
Italy
tel: 00 39 (0) 81 986 237

The Chateau de Vauville
(Palm Trees in Normandy, page 156)
50440 Beaumont-Hague
France
tel: 00 33 (0) 2 33 52 71 11

INDEX

Note: Page numbers in *italics* refer
to captions.

abbey ruins, 115–116, *116*
Abelia grandiflora, 100
Acacia sp., 210
    A. pravissima, 99
    A. verticillata, 111
Acanthus spp., 40, 137, 211
achillea, 172
Aeonium spp., 100, 234
Agapanthus spp., 66, 100, 109, 115,
    128, 129, 140, 147, 218, *218*
    A. praecox orientalis, 111
    A. 'Purple Cloud', 151
Agave spp., 100, 112, 140
alchemilla, 172
Aleppo pine, 19, 72
Allium sp., 172
    A. siculum bulgaricum, 194
almond, *146*
Alocasia macrorrhiza, 143
Aloe sp., 140
    A. arborescens, 111
    A. striatula, 100, 112, *162, 164*
Amaryllis belladona, 112, 136, 214
apple, 122, 124
Aquilegia sp. (colombine), 125
    A. 'Alaska', 154
Araucaria sp., 110
Arbutus spp., 40, 44, 48, 52, 72, 73
Armstrong, Tom, 118–131
Artemisia spp., 40, 140, 152, 154, 172,
    194
    A. arborescens 'Powis Castle', 172
astilbe, 125, 130, 194
Atlantic Ocean
    Block Island (RI), 186, 188–189,
        192
    island off Connecticut, *118, 122,*
        125, 126
    Portugal, 196, 198
    Rhode Island, *168*

Bac, Ferdinand, 64
Bacopa sp., 66
bamboo, *62,* 99, 102–103, *110*
baobab, 214
bayberry, 126

Bay of Saint Laurent, *30*
beech, 74, 99
Berberis 'Aurea', 130
bignonia, 41
boat landing, 168
borage, 116
Borja, Erik, 32–42
Bougainvillea spp., 54, 70, 73, 146,
    147, 183, 203, 211, 214, 222
boxwood, 54, 56, *56, 58, 62,* 124, 127,
    129, *130*
Brandsten, Robert, 74
broom, 72, 122, 158
Brugmansia sanguinea, 108, 110
butterfly bush, 126

Cabot, Frank, 118
cactus, *144,* 214, *214, 224, 226*
Calliandra pulcherrima, 135
Callistemon spp., 112, 147
Calluna vulgaris, 172
Calocedrus decurrens, 136–137
camellia, 135
camphor tree, 70
Canary fern, 135
carastium, 194
carnation, 194
carob tree, 198, *198,* 202
Caruncho, Fernando, 54, 63
Caryopteris sp., 172
castle ruins, 88
casuarina, 147
Catalpa 'Tomentosa', 147
Ceanothus sp., 151
Centaurea sp., 152
cestrum, 73
cherry, 226
chickens, 226, *226*
Choisya spp., 48, *48*
chorisia, 135
Chusqueaculeou 'Breviglumis', 103
Cistus ladanifer, 91
citrus, *26,* 204. *See also specific*
    citrus.
Clematis sp., 122
    C. canadensia, 129
Clianthus puniceus, 114
cloud pruning, 34, *37,* 122
Colcasia spp., *136,* 143
colonnades, 196, 198, 202

columbine, 125, 152
copper beech, 74
Cordyline australis, 100, 111
cork oak, 183
Cosmos sp., 152, 154
crane island, 34, *34*
Crassula sp., 112
crocus, 124
Cryptomeria sp., 40
curves, *66,* 73
Cycas spp., 37, 111, 140, *216,* 218
    C. revoluta, 154
cypress, 19, 26, *26, 30,* 54, 111, 115,
    136, 146, 196, 218

daffodil, 102, *124, 125,* 130
dahlia, 214
datura, 40, 136
Daurauja subspinosa, 114
Davidia involucrata, 103
daylily, 151
delphinium, 154
Dianthus, 194
    D. 'Laced Monarch', 100
Dicksonia, 104
    D. squarrosa, 102
Digitalis, 147
    D. purpurea alba, 154
dining area, 179, 182, 183
dogwood, Japanese, 129
Dornhelm, Robert, 224–229
Dracaena sp., 92, *92*
dry stone river, *34*

Echeveria glauca, 100
Echinops 'Taplow Blue', 172
Echium spp., 66, 104, 109, 111, 115,
    147, 154, *162, 162, 164*
    E. pininana, 98
Elaeagnus, 73, 84
Encephalartos manikensis, 143
Enkianthus chinensis, 194
Erigeron sp., 70
Erythina crista-galli, 136
Escallonia, 84
eucalyptus, 135
Euonymus sp., 84
Euphorbia sp., 152
    E. robbiae, 172
Euryops chrysanthemoides, 110

Faloci, Pierre Louis, 196, 198
ferns, 37, 112, 126, 130, 140, 162
fig, 146, 150, 152, 199, 204
flag garden, 110, 114
flame pruning, 32, 36–37
fountains, 42, 56, 62, 134, 140, 178, 184
Fox, Charles, 98
foxglove, 91
frangipani, 70, 73
fruit trees, 18, 19, 22, 23, 37, 204, 226. See also specific fruits.
Fuchsia spp., 91, 116

Gaillardia spp., 147, 152, 154
garden and landscape unity, 24, 31, 166, 168
gardenia, 37, 66, 73, 183
Gazania sp., 147
    G. spendens, 112
geometric layout, 198, 198, 203
geranium (pelargonium), 66, 91, 146, 147, 150, 151, 152, 199, 203
Geranium maderense, 112, 114
Gestroemia, 66
ginger, 135
Gingko sp., 136
grapefruit, 26, 137
grasses, 40, 166, 168, 172
Grevillea sp., 72
Guillet, Dominique, 144, 146
Gunnera spp., 94, 99, 103, 104, 109, 130, 140, 158, 162

Hamburey family, 106, 108
hammock, 198, 198–199
Hargreaves, George, 74
heather, 72, 172
Hebe spp., 91, 147
Hedychium gardnerianum, 143
heliotrope, 116, 203
hellebore, 130
hens, 226, 226
Hensson, James, 206–209
Hibbert, Eira and Tony, 94–105
Hibiscus spp., 66, 154, 222
Himalayacalamus hookerianus, 102
holly, 84, 99, 106
honey locust, 126
honeysuckle, 41, 130, 137
Hosta spp., 126, 129, 130, 140
house and site integration, 18–19, 24, 40, 44, 48, 230

Hydrangea spp., 70, 99, 102, 126–127, 134, 136, 137, 140, 158, 162
    H. aspera sargentiana, 127
    H. macrophylla 'Mariesii', 40
    H. paniculata 'Grandiflora', 127
    H. petiolaris, 124
    H. quercifolia, 126
    H. seemannii, 82

infinity pool, 218
Innes, Michael, 64, 66
Iris spp., 40, 100, 100, 104, 122, 125, 126, 194
    I. japonica, 84
Isoplexus sceptrum, 112
ivy, 54, 56

jacaranda, 135, 147
Japanese-style gardens, 32–42, 119, 122, 126
jasmine, 37, 48, 48, 70, 73
Jubaea chilensis, 111
Judas tree, 135
juniper, 32, 34, 40, 72, 111

Kunzea baxteri, 112, 112

lamium, 194
Lampranthus sp., 112
landscape and garden unity, 24, 31, 166, 168
Lantana spp., 152, 154
Lapageria sp., 112
larkspur, 194
laurel, 22, 176, 178
Lavandula spp. (lavender), 22, 22, 40, 68, 112, 140, 154, 172, 196, 199
    L. pinnata, 152
lavatera, 154
lavender. See Lavandula.
lawns, 92, 92, 158, 158, 162, 164, 192–193, 216
lemon, 137, 226
Leptospermum scoparium, 147
Leucadendron eucalyptifolium, 84
lilac, 130, 193–194
linden, 124
Lochroma fuchsioides, 114
lotus, 137, 143
lungwort, 129
lupine, 230, 232

Magnolia spp., 62, 73, 99, 103, 129, 135, 136
    M. grandiflora, 136
Manchari, Leila, 208–209, 210, 214
maple, 84, 129, 194
marble column, pink, 58
maritime pine, 19, 40, 72, 126, 152
mastic tree, 40
Mediterranean Sea
    Corsica, 16, 16, 22, 24, 36, 40
    Côte d'Azur, 68, 72, 72–73
    Italy, 136
    Saint-Tropez, 216, 216, 218, 218, 219, 222
    Sardinia, 46, 48, 52, 176, 178, 182, 184, 184
Metrosideros sp., 112, 135
Middleton, Robert, 146
mimosa, 40, 66, 73, 158, 202
Miscanthus sinensis 'Rotsilber', 172
Moore, Henry, 66, 71, 74
myrtle, 22, 26, 40, 72, 147

Nehams, Mike, 109
nicotiana, 154
Niemeyer, Oscar, 64, 66, 73
Norfolk Island pine, 114, 164

oak, 99
Oenothera sp., 152, 152
oleander, 19, 66, 183, 184, 196, 210
Olearia, 84
olive, 19, 24, 26, 30, 40, 72, 152, 196, 198, 210
orange, 26, 137, 210, 226
Osborne, Lynne, 224–229
Osteospermum spp., 100, 112, 115, 152
    O. 'Sunny Ladies', 91

Pachysandra, 124
Pacific Ocean
    Big Sur, 230, 230, 232, 234
    Malibu, 224, 224, 226
    San Francisco, 74, 74
Page, Russell, 132, 140
palm, 54, 72, 92, 92, 98, 98, 104, 110, 111, 114, 114, 140, 151, 156, 162, 162, 210, 214, 218, 218
Palombaggia Gulf, 40
pansy, 203
papyrus, 64, 72, 140, 143, 210
parasol pine, 19, 40

passionflower, 41
pavilion, wooden, *218*, 218–219, *222*
peacocks, *208*, 210
pear, *194*
pedestal, granite, *116*
pelargonium (geranium), *66*,
    91, 146, 147, *150*, 151,
    152, 199, 203
Pellerin, Guillaume, 156–165
peony, tree, 129
pepper tree, 154
pergola, 214
Perone, Paolo, 44, *44*
Perovskia sp., *172*
petunia, 154
Phoenix canariensis, 54, 72, 110, 114,
    114, 151
pine, 22, *42*, 84, *136*
    Aleppo, 19, 72
    maritime, 19, 40, 72, 126, 152
    Norfolk Island, *114*, *164*
    parasol, 19, 40
    umbrella, 99, 152, 196, 218
pinks, 154
Pittosporum spp., 40, 66, 147, 199
plum, 226
Plumbago sp., 147, 203
ponds, 94, 99, *100*
Pontederia sp., 140
pool house, *71*
pools, ornamental, 164, *164*, 202.
        See also ponds; swimming
        pools.
    cross-shaped, with boxwood, 56,
        62, *62*
    with granite fountain, *178*, 184
    half-moon, 202, *204*
    infinity, *218*
    overhanging, 230, 234, *234*
    Russell Page, 140
    solar shaped, *46*, 48
    water lily, *46*, 208, *210*, 210, 214
pots, *66*, *108*
pruning, 36–37, 40, 222
    apple trees, 122, 124
    cloud, *34*, 37, 122
    flame, *32*, 36–37
    in mass, 36
purple beech, 99

rhododendron, 99, 102, *119*, *128*,
    129, 130
rock rose, 40, 91, *116*

Rodgersia tabularis, 130
Roether, Susan, 230
Roman ruins, *206*, 210
Rosa (rose), 112, *118*, 158, 162
    R. 'Baron Girod de l'Ain',
        151
    R. 'La Sharifa Asma', 151
    R. 'New Dawn', 129
    R. *rubiginosa*, 143
    R. *rugosa*, 199, 202
    R. 'Sea Foam', 194
rosemary, 40, 72, 140, 147, 152,
    199, 218

sage, 66, 147, 154, 203
salvia, *172*, 199
sand lily, 210
Santolina spp., *26*, 92, 112, 147
Scabiosa caucasica 'Perfecta Alba',
    154
Schinus molle, 72
Scilla sp., 112
    S. peruviana, 111
sculptures
    Henry Moore, *66*, 71, 74
    raw cement, *24*, 24–25, *30*
    San Francisco sculpture garden,
        74–79
    torso, *58*
Senecio spp., 105, 112
Sequoiadendron gigantium
        (Wellingtonia), 99, 105
shagreen, 22, *23*
shell horn of plenty, *214*
Shigeru Ban, 144
site analysis, 17–18, *34*
Solanum sp., 66
    S. wendlandii, 137
Sollya heterophylla, 151
spindle tree, 73
Spirea spp., *186*, 190, 194
Stachys lanata, 147
stairs, Italian-style, *18*, 22
statice, 147, 154
stone walls, 82, *186*, 186, 194
St. Phalle, Niki de, *218*, 222
structure, 36–37, 196, 198
Styrax obassia, 129
succulents, *224*, 234
sweet pea, 140
swimming pools, 48, *52*, *66*, 68, 71,
        182, 184, *184*, 210, *210*, 218,
        222, 226

tamarisk, *218*, 219, *222*
temples, *208*, 214
terraces, *16*, 18, *18*, 23, 24, *26*, 76, *76*,
    226
terra-cotta urns, *190*
thyme, 92, 146, 154, 199
tortoise island, 34, *34*
Trachymene caerulea, 151
tree fern, 99, 135
tree peony, 129
tulip, *126*, 129
Turckheim, Chloe de, 156–165

umbrella pine, 99, 152, 196, 218

van Sweden, Lassus, 166, 168
vegetable gardens, 45, *45*, 48, 52, 82,
    203–204
Veronica, 168, 172, *172*
Viburnum spp., 98
violet, 203
viperines, *26*

Walling, Christopher, 186–195
Walton, Lady Susanna, 132–143
Walton, Sir William, 132, 140
water channels (water courses), 64,
    66, 70, 71, 72, 202
water lilies, *46*, 140, 143, *208*, 210,
    214
Watsonia sp., 112
Wellingtonia, 99, 105
Westringia fruticosa, 154
Wheelock, Morgan, 122
Wisteria spp., *122*, 129, 203, 226, *226*
wooden bridge, *126*, 130
Woodwardia spp., *137*, 143

yew, 124
Yucca spp., 66, 92, *92*, 100, 110
    Y. gloriosa, 111
Yushania maling, 102–103

zinc ball ornaments, *193*
zinnia, 214
Zsigmond, Vilmos, 230, 234